Water from the Rock
Lutheran Voices from Palestine

Water from the Rock
Lutheran Voices from Palestine

Ann E. Hafften
Contributing Editor

Augsburg Fortress
Minneapolis

WATER FROM THE ROCK
Lutheran Voices from Palestine

Contributing Editor: Ann E. Hafften

Cover design: Koechel Peterson and Associates, Inc., Minneapolis, MN
www.koechelpeterson.com

Cover photos: Lutheran Church of the Reformation in Beit Jala, Palestine: Photo by Mary E. Jensen. Used by permission.
Waterfall: Koechel Peterson and Associates, Inc.

ISBN 0-8066-4989-5

The paper used in this publication meets the minimum requirements of American National Standard for Information Sciences—Permanence of Paper for Printed Library Materials, ANSI Z329.48-1984.

Manufactured in the U.S.A.

07   06   05   04   2   3   4   5   6   7   8   9   10

Contents

Acknowledgments

My dearest hope is that this volume will show readers the faces of Christian brothers and sisters who faithfully live and witness in a land divided by ceaseless struggle. They bring us the gospel from an unexpected place. If we listen, they will be Jesus for us, the water of life.

I am grateful to people who have taught me that love and friendship cross borders and bridge cultures: the lay people and pastors of Bethlehem and Beit Sahour and all the people of the Evangelical Lutheran Church in Jerusalem; the members of Kibbutz Kfar Menachem; my coworkers in the Evangelical Lutheran Church in America—Sandra Holloway, the Rev. Said Ailabouni, and the Rev. Eric Shafer; and the caring people of the ELCA who are finding ways to pray and work for peace.

I thank and honor my husband, the Rev. Franz Schemmel, my parents—Donna Wiethoff and the late Carl Hafften—and my outstanding community of friends.

Introduction

Lutherans in Palestine? Yes—and they are a blessing to us! As God brought water from a rock for Moses and his wandering people when hope seemed impossible, these Arab brothers and sisters bring the gospel to us from an unexpected source. They remind the world of the way God brought life from death.

When I speak or teach in congregations I encounter wide-eyed surprise at the news that there are Arab Palestinians who are Christian—and who are Lutheran. It's true. Palestinian Christians—Palestinian Lutherans—trace their heritage in the body of Christ to New Testament days.

If you are a Christian in the West Bank or Gaza, you are a Palestinian. They are sometimes called the invisible—or the forgotten—Christians.

Well-meaning Americans often ask Palestinian Lutherans, "When did you convert to Christianity?" or "When did your family become Christian?" In the book of Acts, Luke mentions "Arabs" in his account of those who were gathered at the event of the first Pentecost (Acts 2:8-12). Christians have been a faithful community in the Middle East since then.

Palestinian Christians—actually, all Palestinians—are often lumped into the stereotype of Palestinians as terrorists. The Lutherans of Palestine are dedicated to proclaiming God's love in Jesus! They are committed to providing vital education and health ministries. They are not extremists, though they are passionate about the injustice of life under an illegal occupation. Lutheran leaders speak boldly for peace and they have much to teach us of justice.

Christians have lived in the Holy Land for hundreds of years in harmony with Muslim and Jewish neighbors. As a minority group, they make a distinct contribution to the work of peacemaking in the region. Yet Palestinian Christian voices are not often heard in the media or in American churches. The clamor of Middle East violence and controversy, together with the dominance in the U.S. popular media of evangelical "Christian Zionists," almost completely drown them out.

This book seeks to make the voices of Palestinian Lutherans heard in the United States. The Lutheran voices presented here describe the experience of displacement; of refugee status; of fear; loss and grief; of life under an oppressive occupation. In pain, they also speak to the possibility of hope and peace with justice.

It is important to note that these writings have all come to us since the September 2000 beginning of the resistance and conflict known as the second *Intifada*. This Palestinian uprising (and the Israeli response) grew out of collapsed hopes for the Oslo Peace Accords and the continued seizure of Palestinian land for illegal Israeli settlements. On top of that came the people's outrage at Ariel Sharon's provocative trip in the company of a large military contingent to the complex of sacred Muslim mosques in Jerusalem called the *Haram al-Sharif*, known to Jews as the "Temple Mount."

Christians make up about eight percent of the population in the West Bank, with numbers totaling around 50,000. (Another 100,000 Christians are citizens of Israel.) Members of the Greek Orthodox Church make up the biggest group of Christians, with Copts, Syrian Orthodox, Armenian Orthodox, Roman Catholics, and Greek Catholic Christians all in the mix. Protestant churches include the Anglican, Lutheran, Baptist, and Nazarene, plus a number of independent evangelical groups.

The Evangelical Lutheran Church in Jerusalem (ELCJ) was formed in 1959, though the history of Lutherans in the Holy Land goes back 150 years. The 2,000 ELCJ members are in six congregations, located in Bethlehem, Beit Jala, Beit Sahour, Ramallah, Jerusalem, and Amman (Jordan).

These congregations work hard to serve their struggling communities. Five of them operate schools that serve children from all denominations, and about 30 percent of the students are Muslim.

Augusta Victoria Hospital, a ministry of the Lutheran World Federation, provides critical health care services from its location on the Mount of Olives and through mobile clinics that move among the villages of the West Bank. My church, the Evangelical Lutheran Church in America (ELCA), supports the ELCJ with funding and missionary pastors.

Too often, the five West Bank congregations are virtually walled in by Israeli-imposed closures. Checkpoints and curfews restrict movement in and among West Bank communities, severely hampering the churches' ability to carry out their ministries. But rather than give in to defeat or bitter partisanship, the Lutherans persist in their call to peacemaking. Both the native Palestinians and the international Lutherans who live and work among that community provide a radiant witness to grace in the midst of conflict.

Viola Raheb, then director of schools for the Evengelical Lutheran Church in Jerusalem, was outspoken in 2001 when she told the ELCA assembly that U.S. Lutherans should not worry so much about whose side they are on in the Middle East. "Instead, get on the side of those who are working for peace! They are Palestinians and Israelis, Christians, Jews, and Muslims," she said.

In a land of conflict, the ELCJ has a special ministry of reconciliation among people victimized by war. The church is committed to nonviolence. Nonviolence education is incorporated in the curriculum of all the Lutheran schools, combined with a focus on working together for peace in a diverse cultural community. The ELCJ and its bishop, the Rev. Munib Younan, participate in dialogue among Christians, Jews, and Muslims for peace and truth, and Bishop Younan has an important role among Jerusalem's Christian leadership.

My own audiences, puzzled by the complexities of the Middle East conflict, always ask me where to find hope. I feel strongly that our hope can be renewed if we will see the humanity and receive the profound gospel insight of our Palestinian Christian brothers and sisters.

At the Lutheran Church of the Redeemer in Jerusalem's Old City, the congregation says, "We live in the Resurrection neighborhood." The church is only steps away from the traditional site of Jesus' crucifixion and resurrection. Its members bring a note of resurrection hope to every discussion of conflict and peacemaking. We are blessed when we hear their voices and glimpse their hearts.

When we address the concerns of Palestinians and struggle with issues around the state of Israel, questions are inevitably raised about the Lutheran church's relations with the Jewish people. The ELCA has an important program of Lutheran/Jewish dialogue underway, an area for which the ELCA Department for Ecumenical Affairs has provided strong leadership. I feel that we must trust the integrity of that relationship, but we should not fail to hear these prophetic voices from Palestine or speak ourselves when we see injustice.

While I have made 13 trips to the Middle East, I was slow to come to know the Palestinian Christian community. I first visited Jerusalem and the holy shrines in 1977 as a student of art and the history of the church. Like most pilgrim groups, we accepted the maps handed out at the airport by the Israeli Ministry of Tourism, and we were completely unaware of the Palestinian population or our transit in and out of the Occupied Territories. The next year I returned to live and work for six months on a kibbutz, or collective farm, in Israel.

As a teenager in the 1960s, I was fascinated with the Zionist movement and the romance of the young state of Israel. My extended stay in Israel allowed me to meet some of the real people of the story. I am grateful for the lifelong guidance of these Israeli friends who showed me the beauty of their ideals and their love of the land, and in recent years their acute disappointment in the outcome of their dream. Learning the truth of their lives complicated my naïve, mythic understanding of Israel.

Gradually I learned how thousands of Palestinian people became refugees in the 1948 *Nakbah*, or "catastrophe." Christian and Muslim Arabs fled radical Jewish terrorism or were forcibly driven away as the state of Israel came into being. It was a time when villages were destroyed and a society was forced into exile that lasts until this day. Among those Christians were the parents and grandparents of today's Palestinian Lutherans.

In the years that followed my stay in Israel, I visited the region as often as I could. I became aware of the Lutheran church in the West Bank while I was on the national staff of the former American Lutheran Church, and by 1988 I had become acquainted with Palestinian and Israeli peace activists.

In 1989, two years into the first Palestinian *Intifada*, I took part in a solidarity delegation sponsored by the Fellowship of Reconciliation. During the season when Israel's soldiers were ordered to break the bones of Palestinians, we were present to observe nonviolent resistance. We found determination and grace in the work of activists in the West Bank and Gaza, and in the hearts of the Palestinian families that opened their homes to us, Christians in Beit Sahour and Muslims in Gaza.

Since then I have been continually blessed by contact with the Palestinian members of my own church—the Lutheran church. I am grateful for the congregations and the leaders of the Evangelical Lutheran Church in Jerusalem. In the midst of destruction, oppression, and suffering, theirs is a witness of patience, of hope for justice, of trust in the promises of Christ.

Lutherans in the Middle East ask for the prayers of U.S. Christians, for our help in telling the truth of their story, and for our advocacy efforts on behalf of peace for all the people of Israel and Palestine. The Lutheran voices in this volume can inspire and equip us for those tasks.

The voices you will encounter here are lay and clergy leaders in the Evangelical Lutheran Church in Jerusalem (ELCJ) and Lutheran missionaries serving in the Palestinian community.

The Rev. Munib A. Younan is the bishop of the ELCJ, the leader of a small protestant church in a setting where most Christian churches are orthodox and Christians are a distinct minority. He has been called to a unique role among church leaders in the region, including initiating interfaith dialogue in Jerusalem. He is a leader in the Middle East Council of Churches, the Lutheran World Federation, and the Fellowship of the Middle East Evangelical Churches. Munib Younan received his early education in the Lutheran schools of Jerusalem and Beit Jala, and he studied at the Al-Ahlia College in Ramallah. He studied deaconry and theology at Jarvenpaa, Finland, and the University of Helsinki, Finland. Pastor Younan has served three ELCJ congregations. He is the author of *Witnessing for Peace: In Jerusalem and the World* (Minneapolis: Fortress Press, 2003).

Viola Raheb is a Palestinian Lutheran educator and advocate for peace. A native of Bethlehem, Viola Raheb worked as superintendant of the Lutheran school system. She graduated from Ruprecht-Karls University in Germany with an M.A. in education and theology. Viola Raheb lives in Vienna, Austria.

The Rev. Mary E. Jensen is a pastor of the Evangelical Lutheran Church in America, working in Jerusalem through the Division for Global Mission. She serves the Evangelical Lutheran Church in Jerusalem as communications assistant to Bishop Munib Younan. She is the author, together with Father Elias Chacour, of *We Belong to the Land: The Story of a Palestinian Israeli Who Lives for Peace and Reconciliation* (New York: HarperCollins, 1992).

Dr. Nuha Khoury has been back in Palestine since 1996 working as the Deputy Director of the Dar al-Kalima Academy project of the International Center of Bethlehem. A native of Bethlehem, she earned a Ph.D. in Islamic history from the University of Michigan at Ann Arbor.

The Rev. Mitri Raheb is the pastor of Evangelical Christmas Lutheran Church in Bethlehem, in the occupied West Bank. His church endured 40 days of curfew by the Israeli Defense Force in the spring of 2002. A native of Bethlehem, he is also the founder of the International Center of Bethlehem and the Dar al-Kalima Model School and Academy. He is the author of *I am a Palestinian Christian* (Minneapolis: Fortress Press, 1995) and *Bethlehem 2000: Past and Present* (Northampton, MA: Interlink Publishing, 1998).

The Revs. Michael and Susan Thomas were called in the summer of 1998 by the ELCA Division for Global Mission to serve the English-speaking congregation of the Lutheran Church of the Redeemer in the Old City, Jerusalem. They worked closely with the Evangelical Lutheran Church of Jerusalem. Prior to coming to Jerusalem they served the international parish at Vienna, Austria. In late 2002, Susan began serving as pastor of Our Savior Lutheran Church and Student Center and as Lutheran Chaplain at Dartmouth College in Hanover, New Hampshire. Michael will complete his service in Jerusalem in the summer of 2003 and join her to serve as co-pastor there.

Ann E. Hafften

1

Bishop Munib Younan

The Rev. Munib A. Younan is the bishop of the Evangelical Lutheran Church in Jerusalem (ELCJ). In his book, *Witnessing for Peace in Jerusalem and the World* (Minneapolis: Fortress Press, 2003), Bishop Younan writes about how he came to understand his identity as a Palestinian Christian. His was a family of refugees, drastically affected by the Catastrophe of 1948. In this period, both Christians and Muslims either fled radical Jewish violence or were driven away by the military as the state of Israel came into being.

The bishop's father was an exile from Beersheba living in Jerusalem at that time. His mother's family lived in the western part of Jerusalem, but the family fled to the Old City when they were ordered out of their home. So Munib Younan grew up within the ancient walls, his family struggling to survive. His mother was insistent that the children receive an education and went to work herself to make it happen. She had attended the Lutheran Talitha Kumi School for girls, and the family sent Munib Younan to a Lutheran school as well. As a youth, Munib Younan wanted to become a pastor, but there were few resources for developing young leadership.

While Younan was in a vocational holding pattern, the church hired the future bishop to work as the doorkeeper. If you go to the Lutheran Church of the Redeemer today, a doorkeeper will greet you and show you to the steps of the tower, which provides one of the best views in the city.

In 1969 an opportunity came to 18-year-old Munib Younan when he was invited to meet with two men from Finland who had an educational scholarship to offer. Within months, he was alone in Finland, studying the language and preparing to enter college. He studied there for seven years, earning both a bachelor's and a master's degree.

Younan came into contact with Israeli officials during his first year in Finland, when his visa had to be renewed. The effect of a life under occupation was enough to make the experience terrifying. His situation was complicated by the fact that such visas normally were issued in Israel. Younan found that the first secretary of the Embassy wanted to help him because Younan was a Christian. Italian Catholics had hidden this Jewish official during the war and saved his life.

⌐ Bishop Younan's Reformation Day Message ⌐

I will greatly rejoice in the LORD, my whole being shall exult in my God; for he has clothed me with the garments of salvation, he has covered me with the robe of righteousness, as a bridegroom decks himself with a garland, and as a bride adorns herself with her jewels. For as the earth brings forth its shoots, and as a garden causes what is sown in it to spring up, so the Lord GOD will cause righteousness and praise to spring up before all the nations.

⌐ *Isaiah 61:10-11*

As I read this proclamation of salvation and righteousness by the prophet Isaiah, I felt elevated out of this world. When I read that "the Lord has clothed me with the garments of salvation and has covered me with the robe of righteousness," I thought I had begun to live in an idealistic place of justice and salvation. I felt revived in the same spirit as in the sixth century B.C., when the hopes of liberation were being realized, when the Israelites' hopes of liberation were being realized.

But alas, the reality of our tough, unjust world immediately struck me. One of my Jewish rabbi friends asked me last week, "Bishop, do you think there is a future for justice in our country?" My answer was as always, "As long as we believe in a living God, there is hope."

A Christian woman visited me last week too, and she adamantly emphasized that the solution for the Middle East is spiritual before being "secular," to use her exact words.

Between these two stories, I started to feel the tension of this Reformation Day. I started to struggle, like the reformer Martin Luther, to find the gracious God. I started to feel the tension that exists between God's salvation—God's justification for human beings by grace without works or merit—and the implications of justice in our broken world. But again I was reminded that justification by grace through faith is closely associated with the search for justice.

As we look back in the Old Testament, we find that justice is grounded in God's divine nature. This has far-reaching implications for righteous living, righteous judging, and righteous rejoicing. The worship expected of the righteous, the one who practices justice and righteousness, stems from obedience to the Covenant. Professor von Rad says that there is no concept more important in the Hebrew Scriptures than justice.

When Isaiah called the people of Israel to repent and come back to their covenant relationship with God, they were reminded that it would mean seeking justice and correcting oppression (Isaiah 1:17), letting the oppressed go free, breaking every yoke (Isaiah 58:6). The prophet Micah spells out what God is really looking for from those who have covenanted to be a blessing: "What does the LORD require of you but to do justice, and to love kindness, and to walk humbly with your God?" (Micah 6:8).

The New Testament perspective of justice is rooted in the procla-mation and inauguration of the reign of God in the person of Jesus Christ. In the Gospel of St. Luke, Jesus sets out his program, his purpose, and his message of salvation, including the mission of jus-tice. "The Spirit . . . has sent me . . . to let the oppressed go free" (Luke 4:18). In the Gospel of St. Matthew, Jesus reminds the reli-gious leaders that they had given too much attention to ritual purity and neglected the weightier matter of justice (Matthew 23:23).

Dr. Ishmael Noko, General Secretary of the Lutheran World Federation, explains the relationship between justice and justifica-tion: It is a call to all those who are baptized into Christ to take part in building community across the barriers that exist between nations, ethnic groups, genders, and generations. Because we are justified by God and not by our own qualities or actions, we should all receive one another as God receives us. The gift of justification that we receive in Christ is an affirmation that we are all made in God's image, that we are each of value as an individual.

Being justified by grace through faith returns us to the real meaning of biblical justice. It describes the ambiguity in which we human beings find ourselves. We are at the same time sinners and saints, always in need of justice and liberation, which God graciously gives us. It means simultaneously being judged and being freed. Those of us experiencing injustice in this world have the promise of the wonderful hope of justice from the cross and resurrection of Christ. Yes, we are victims of injustice, but as we are saved by God's grace, the triune God will never allow injustice to have the final word. Justice and only justice will have that final word.

What my guest told me is true—the crisis of justice is spiritual. As long as human beings are far from God, then true justice is far from the world. As long as justice is deeply rooted in self-interest, economy, and power, then God's justification has no value for true justice. As long as justice has double or triple standards, then it contradicts the power of the cross.

This is true justice: that God has redeemed all humanity equally, regardless of gender, ethnicity, or race, whether powerful or weak, rich or poor, from the North or South, East or West.

The justice of our modern world is dividing the world's peoples and countries into an "axis of evil" in contrast to an "axis of good." This division is a challenge to religious communities and to our understanding of humanity. We need to analyze it, to discuss it in a constructive way. When people and nations are said to be a part of an "axis of evil" we must ask ourselves, "What is behind such language? Is the Northern world trying to create religious, ethnic, and theological polarizations that threaten to divide the world's people into a number of warring camps, each possessed by the need to dominate through fear?"

The editor of the ELCA's magazine *The Lutheran*, the Rev. David L. Miller, writes: "(The rhetoric) we are hearing simplistically defines nations in terms of our (American) needs, fear, and anger. It fixes the identity of entire peoples as essentially opposed to us, ignoring their needs, legitimate aspirations and groups within their societies with whom we share values and interests." (*The Lutheran*, May 2002)

The rhetoric of the "axis of evil" stimulates war fever to convince people that military options against the bad group are the only way of dealing with destructive leaders and governments. It depersonalizes entire peoples so we no longer see them, lest we notice the destruction that our national policies wreak on nations that are being demonized.

Unfortunately, the rhetoric of "axis of evil" blinds the world to justice and to the reality that life is interconnected. No person or nation is an island. Our Creator fashions a unity in which each element is connected with the others.

For these reasons, justification by grace through faith proclaims that the compassion of God has no respect for the world's judgment of purity, acceptability, or net worth. "All have sinned and fall short of the glory of God; they are now justified by his grace as a gift, through the redemption that is in Christ Jesus" (Romans 3:23-24). God's mercy is for sinners, both in the "axis of evil" and the "axis of good," rich as Zacchaeus and poor as Lazarus at the gate. The justice of God is seen in Jesus who died on the cross for all people equally and freely.

Where politicians see barriers, the Christian church finds companions with whom it can join to oppose the barbarism of death, destruction, and demonization. United in its opposition, the church becomes the "axis of hope" created by the Spirit, sharing in God's loving dream for all peoples and the whole creation. Wherever the church finds people truly affirming the sacredness of life, there we find the Spirit of Life at work creating an axis of hope. The mercy of God's future appears, creating a spiral—not of violence, but of life—working for justice that alone holds the promise of peace in our world.

By saying this, I believe that justification by grace through faith calls the church to be prophetic and even to swim against the waves of injustice in our world. Professor Dietrich Bonhoeffer put it this way: "It is part of the Church's office of guardianship that it shall call sin by its name and that she shall warn men [and women] against sin; for 'righteousness exalteth a nation,' both in time and in eternity." (*Ethics*, New York: The Macmillen Company, 1961, p. 314.)

If the church does not do this, it would be incurring part of the guilt for the blood of the wicked (see Ezekiel 3:17). Only justice will save the world and humanity from wars, calamities and bloodshed.

The Palestinian Church is also called to be an axis of hope and to be prophetic. It is called to condemn injustice but at the same time to bring hope, work for justice, and prepare a generation of hope and peace. We do this by treating people justly at home and at work, raising our children to trust in Jesus Christ as our Savior, living just and peaceful lives. We do this by teaching justice and peace in our Lutheran and Christian schools, and practicing justice, peace, and reconciliation in our congregations. It is the call of the church to condemn oppression, occupation, and violence in our country, but at the same time to call for just peace for both Israel and Palestine according to international legitimacy.

The Christian church needs to be prophetic in order to break the vicious cycle of hatred and revenge. Justification by grace through faith calls the Palestinian Church not only to work for justice but also to be ministers of reconciliation in our homes, our congregations, and in this land. We are to educate the grassroots of both nations to see God not only in oneself but also in the other, whom we consider to be an enemy. Once we see God in the other, then we can accept the humanity of the other and even the otherness of the other. Once the humanity of the other is rediscovered, then we can mutually recognize each other's human, civil, religious, national, and political rights. Only then will our country, Palestine and Israel, become a promised land of milk and honey for both Palestinians and Israelis.

I conclude my message on this Reformation Day by quoting Dr. Martin Luther King Jr. Today I am sure Dr. King's language would be inclusive, speaking of both men and women, but I am sharing this quotation from the 1960s exactly as it was spoken:

> When evil men plot, good men must plan.
> When evil men burn and bomb, good men must build and bind.
> When evil men shout ugly words of hatred, good men must commit themselves to the glories of love.
> When evil men seek to perpetuate an unjust status quo, good men must seek to bring into being a real order of justice.

May the peace of our Lord Jesus Christ fill your hearts and minds and souls with the gracious love of God. Amen

Jerusalem, October 31, 2002

— Bishop Munib Younan's Christmas Message 2002 —

But the angel said to [the shepherds], "Do not be afraid; for see—I am bringing you good news of great joy for all the people: to you is born this day in the city of David a Savior who is the Messiah, the Lord."

∾ *Luke 2:10-11*

Christmas and fear do not go together, but the beautiful Christmas story in the Gospel of Luke shows us three kinds of human fear. The angel told the shepherds, "Do not be afraid." This message of hope and courage was given to everyone in the Christmas story and is given to us today, wherever we are.

First, there was the fear that expected the Savior. Mary certainly experienced fear hearing the astounding message of the Angel Gabriel, and in her pregnancy, in her concerns about where her child would be born, in the reality of no room for the Savior at the inn at Bethlehem.

Joseph, too, undoubtedly experienced fear when he learned of Mary's pregnancy, as he determined to divorce her quietly; in the message of the angel that told him the truth about Mary's pregnancy and asked him to love and care for her and the babe.

And the shepherds in the fields near Beit Sahour were in the darkness when they saw strange signs in the heavens and became extremely afraid, falling to the ground. The angel's message began with words of comfort and hope: "Do not be afraid."

Secondly, there was the fear that expected a rival to existing power. King Herod was fearful because he heard that a rival king had been born. In his fear he was determined to destroy that rival, eventually using death as collective punishment against the small children of Bethlehem.

In our modern, globalized world, we know the King Herod kind of fear. We see firsthand the struggles for power that make nations afraid of each other, driving them to fight each other and legitimize war. This kind of fear does not give a glimmer of hope.

Today I am asking: Why should the Palestinian people in the Holy Land live in such fear under Israeli military occupation? Fear of violence, of bloodshed, of curfews, of checkpoints, of siege, of walls of separation? Why do we have to fear whether or not Palestinian schools and universities will be open, if it is possible to go to work to earn a basic living, or even if it is safe to leave one's home?

Why should an Israeli live in fear, even though Israel holds the power in our country? I know that fear is the common denominator for both Israelis and Palestinians because all are afraid of what the future holds for them and their children. Is the Christmas message that we should be afraid, like Herod, taking measures that are destructive and create more fear and more insecurity? Fear can drive people to frustration. This frustration can create religious and political extremism. We are fed up in this country with every kind of extremism or fanaticism.

There is no conflict on this earth of which world leaders know the root cause and the solution so well as they do the Israeli-Palestinian conflict. Why then are there no charismatic world leaders who will relieve the peoples of this land from ongoing suffering and injustice? Why are there no world leaders ready to pluck out the fear of the peoples by implementing the international legitimacy; allowing the two-state solution to be realized and practiced; recognizing that security for Israelis is dependent on freedom and justice for the Palestinians? Only when this happens will the angel's message be clearly heard by all the peoples in this land: "Do not be afraid."

The third fear in the Christmas story was the natural fear of destructive political realities. Mary, Joseph, the shepherds, and even the Magi had natural, legitimate reasons to fear King Herod and the Roman military occupation. They were struggling with problems of daily living, and with being coerced to register with the Roman authorities and heavily taxed by Rome, with the ever-present

Roman soldiers, with the well-known destructiveness of King Herod, with the inability to see a hopeful future. In the Christmas story we hear that the Magi took another way home, fearing the anger of King Herod against themselves and the Christ child. We also hear that the holy family escaped from King Herod's murderous anger by taking refuge in another country, seeking life, safety, and a future.

As we celebrate Christmas in the midst of military occupation, Palestinians live in daily fear. It is certainly this fear that is driving some Palestinian Christians to emigrate from the holy land, leaving a small community of Christians to remain here. It is painful to see the proliferation of emigration just when we want and need the people to stay in the land. What is the Holy Land without the baptized people of the land?

Sisters and brothers, the Christmas story tells us that fear did not stop Mary from proceeding in faith to give birth to the Savior of the world. Fear did not stop Joseph from loving and caring for Mary and the Child in great faith. Fear did not quash the hope and joy of the shepherds nor stop them from seeking the Messiah, born in Bethlehem. We know times when we feel that God is remote from us; perhaps we even feel abandoned by our Savior. Our spirituality may falter. But God is with us—Emmanuel. We can count on the presence of our Savior, Jesus the Christ.

We will refuse to let our fears drive us to escapism, racism, xenophobia, revenge, or extremism. Our fears will never stop us from being God's instruments for a just peace, apostles of love and ministers of reconciliation. I call on people of good conscience and good will from both nations, Palestine and Israel, and the three religions—Judaism, Christianity and Islam—to intensify their efforts to end the occupation, violence, destruction, bloodshed, and death. I call on them to incarnate just peace and reconciliation in this land which so desperately needs and deserves it.

The fears of Mary, Joseph, the shepherds, and the Magi teach us to remain faithful and to seek the Savior, clinging to God's promises of good news and great joy in Christ. Political solutions are certainly necessary and welcome, but as Palestinian Christians we recognize the power of God to change the world through the gift and birth of the Savior who is the Messiah, the Lord. Our Savior is more powerful than kings, presidents, governments, soldiers, and military powers.

Christ rejuvenates in us the motivation and the strength to work for justice, peace, and reconciliation against all odds. The Babe reminds us that whatever military or punitive actions may be taken, whatever harassments we experience, one thing is sure: Only the birth of the Prince of Peace brings to us a different kind of peace, a different kind of justice, a different kind of reconciliation, not the peace, justice, or reconciliation of the world.

As dark and bleak as everything may seem, our hope only lies in the birth of our Savior. Let us offer our hearts as a manger for the Christ child, receiving God's holy gifts in Word and Sacrament. Let us join together to pray to our loving God, asking that our fears be taken away and our faith be strengthened. Prayer can do so much more than we think or imagine. Jesus, when cleansing a boy from a devastating illness, said that it was only by prayer and fasting that the child would be healed and released (Mark 9:29), and this also corresponds to Palestine and Israel. "Do not be afraid." We thank God for his healing and wholeness in Christ.

Come, Lord Jesus, and take away our paralysis of fear. Use us as your instruments of love and peace, justice, and reconciliation, now at Christmas and always. Amen

Jerusalem, December 23, 2002

Questions for reflection and discussion

1. Can you imagine becoming a refugee: fleeing your home as a child or trying to assemble your children for a race to safety far from home? Palestinian families were separated during the chaos of 1948. Others came together, married, and raised families as refugees. What do you imagine to be some of the feelings and challenges that face refugees?

2. Justification by grace through faith is important to Lutherans. Do you ever think about being justified or what it means? In what ways is justification about being okay with God and with each other? In what ways is justification also about justice and injustice in the world?

3. Bishop Younan speaks of those who experience injustice in this world, including his people, the Palestinians. What do you think it means that God will not allow injustice to have the final word?

4. The world's understanding of justice would divide people into an "axis of evil" and an "axis of good." Is this how God expects us to understand humanity?

5. Bishop Younan asks, "Why should the Palestinian people live in fear under Israeli military occupation? Why should an Israeli live in fear, even though Israel holds the power?" In what ways do you think fear is the common denominator for both Israelis and Palestinians? What do you think are some of their common fears?

6. What does it take to refuse to let fear drive us to escapism, racism, xenophobia, revenge, or extremism? The bishop says fear should never keep his people from being God's instruments for a just peace, apostles of love, and ministers of reconciliation. What about us?

2

Viola Raheb

Viola Raheb is a Palestinian Lutheran educator and advocate for peace.

⌐ Forgiveness, Reconciliation, and Renewal: Our Forgotten Sisters in Palestine ⌐

In January 2002, Viola Raheb spoke with Lutheran Woman Today, *the bimonthly publication of Women of the ELCA, about daily life in the Middle East and the hopes of those who dare to dream.*

Where did you grow up?

I was born in Bethlehem in 1969 to a small Palestinian Christian Lutheran family. I lived the majority of my life there until I went to do my studies in Germany. We're a small family in a Palestinian context—myself and one older brother, who is pastor of Christmas Lutheran Church in Bethlehem. I've been back in Palestine, working there, since 1995.

What was your childhood like?

I grew up well. I was born after the occupation of 1967, so I grew up within the context of occupation. A military presence has always been a part of life—seeing heavily equipped soldiers all over the place.

When I was growing up, it was forbidden to use the word "Palestine" or to get to know anything about our own history, to know anything of our literature or lyrics. It was forbidden to read books on Palestine.

I lived on the small street where I'm back now. It is next to the Church of the Nativity, and it's the route all pilgrims take when they come to the Holy Land. I grew up hearing Christmas carols even in the middle of August. It shaped my picture of what pilgrims are looking for—and are never able to find because they are looking in the wrong place for it.

I finished high school in 1987, when the first *Intifada* (uprising) started. Schools were closed down for almost three years, and I started teaching in homes so the children would not be illiterate. Then I went to Germany for six years and came back when the peace process started. And now again, I am living in the context of a second *Intifada*.

I really never had a childhood in the sense you would know in the States. I grew up much quicker than I would have loved to. I didn't have a childhood where I could just be innocent and play. Politics was our daily bread. This shaped me and my childhood memories to a very large extent.

Was that the most influential part of growing up, or do other things stand out?

One of the things that really impacted me was when two classmates were jailed for a year for reading Palestinian literature. We were 16. I couldn't comprehend what wrong they did to be sentenced to jail just for reading a book. Then one of the two was assassinated in the first *Intifada*.

It was too early—at 16, you're not at an age to realize what risk means. It hits you so hard that all of a sudden your whole world collapses. And then you ask yourself, "Where is my place in all of this?" This was one of the things that made me decide to do what I'm doing now, advocacy work. I know it is so important to make people know the story and not be silenced by the media.

It gave you the lens that you see things through.

It made me realize that you have to ask yourself whether you want your soul to die under occupation, and just be concerned about the dishwashing and the cooking, or whether you want to hold on to who you are in your inner self. And with that, maybe to risk so many things that matter to you.

Can you share with us your perspective of the way things are among the people of Palestine, their intentions and their everyday lives?

I think the most difficult thing to make people understand is what occupation really means. It's so far from reality in the States. Occupation for me is not so much an issue of the military presence. It's about living in a country where you cannot travel except if you have a permit to do so, where you cannot go back to your home country unless you have a permit to do so. Where you can lose your citizenship if you stay longer than the permit allows you. Occupation is about living in a city where my freedom of movement is limited to a two-kilometer radius, where often I cannot even visit friends or family members because the road would just end with a blockade or an Israeli military checkpoint.

Occupation for me is about living in a country where water is a political tool, where we get water once every two or three weeks. It is about people who cannot get medical treatment because Israeli checkpoints prohibit them from reaching hospitals in Jerusalem. It's about not being able to work in my office (which is only eight kilometers away from where I live) for the last six years. Occupation for me is about being harassed at every checkpoint and at the airport just for being who I am.

In the last few months it's been about not being able to sleep because bombings go on from early afternoon until early morning. It's about a context where everything you own can be confiscated, and you can do nothing about it.

What really matters about occupation is that it goes right to the heart of basic human rights in everyday life. People are not so concerned about politics—they are concerned about being able to go to work. At the moment we have 80 percent unemployment in Bethlehem—not because the people don't have jobs, but because they either cannot get to their jobs or they live on tourism, and there is currently no tourism.

This is what daily life is about. If you sleep, then you wake up wondering, how am I going to survive this thing? Will there be water? Will they cut off the electricity? The telephone lines? How far can I get today with my car? Can I get the supplies that I need, the medical treatment I need? Will my children come safe home from school, or will there be bombing before they return home? These are the kinds of things that matter in our circumstances.

It's about not being able to plan. Here in the States you plan for years ahead, but I can't plan what I will do tomorrow. And so I live from moment to moment, which makes life even harder. We don't know what will be possible. I have left home and then found out that all possibilities of going back are blocked. I can't think about five days ahead when I'm just trying to get back home.

It must be an exhausting way to live. How do you cling to hope?

It's tough to live in the context we live in. It makes me sad to see that people don't know what we are going through. It makes me more sad that they don't know that we are there. You feel left alone, trying not to drown in the midst of all this hopelessness.

This is why I think it is important to see sometimes that hope is not something you can preach about, where people get it like an adrenaline rush and they are so happy and thrilled—this is not about that. This is about something that keeps you waking up every morning, makes you go to work in spite of all that is happening around you.

Because we only know what the media tell us, it's important to talk about this with you. What do you think is possible or achievable for the future of Israel and Palestine?

One has to distinguish between short-term and long-term. This is very hard, because we want to have something tangible to look to and say, "in five years, in two years, this is what will happen." What keeps me going is to know that it's like the parable of the one who was planting seeds. This is all that we can do—plant seeds. We cannot predict if they will fall in good soil, if there will be enough rain, if they will ever bear fruit, or if they will ever make it.

In the short term, I think we're heading toward an apartheid system. I also think the situation will escalate. One plan that has been discussed is to divide the West Bank into 56 small homelands for Palestinians surrounded by Israeli settlements—disconnected from each other, and so economically with no future. So if I were to look only at this, I don't think I would see any reason to continue being—not only there, but just being in general, because that is where I see myself at home.

In the long run, I think there is no other solution but to have both nations and all three religions find a way to coexist, to accept that wanting the right of existence for oneself is directly connected to the right of existence for the other. If it excludes anyone, it will not be possible. I think in the long run, there is no other way but to have two states or two nations that exist next to each other. Many people think this is a naive vision, but it's not about loving one another—it's about accepting you even if I cannot love you. Not loving you doesn't mean I need to hit you or kill you.

There is no other way but to learn to survive together, not because we want to or even because we will be better human beings for it but because the challenges we will be facing will make us have to. At the moment, water is a political tool. But we also know that in a few years there will be no water: It will either be gone or not good for human use. One state alone will not be able to find the solution. So the challenges that are ahead of us are forcing us to think more regionally and globally.

People think Israelis and Palestinians are so different, and that's why we cannot understand each other. I believe that we are very similar, to an extent that is frightening for many people—that's why it is so difficult to accept the other, because you see part of yourself when you look at the other. I think we need, as in psychotherapy, to acknowledge that we have a problem in order to be able to solve it.

At the moment, we're in the stage of denial, hoping that it will solve itself. And so the treatment is a very long process. It can only start when we recognize that we do really have something to work on.

What keeps me going is that even if I will not live to see it, maybe the generation of my children or my grandchildren will experience peaceful coexistence. But the only way for them to experience that is if I commit myself to it today.

Readers are going to want to know if there is any way they can help you achieve this vision.

It's very important to work with the young generation at home. This is why I'm in the field of education. Those 12 to 15 years really shape you. It shapes whether you will be a citizen, or in a dictator's regime, whether you learn to accept everything or whether you will be somebody who thinks critically and dares to challenge and question what is happening, to make an impact. I think that we can give hope to the young generation that it is worthwhile to invest in their country and in themselves. Then we will have done a great deal for realizing that long-term process. If we can help them to see God's creation in the other, not dehumanizing the other, then we have done a great deal for reconciliation. And if we can help people to learn to plant trees at a time when bulldozers are pulling up trees, then I think we are giving peace a chance to become a reality.

When it comes to the United States, especially the women, what I hope for is that they know that we do exist as their sisters, their often forgotten sisters. It hurts to be forgotten. Secondly, I wish for women to reach out to these sisters—not only to know that they exist but to reach out to them. I think there is much that can be done, whether it's connecting organizations to women's groups, to churches, to women's magazines, or whatever. Thirdly, what is important is that women view this as a mutual relationship, because often people think that being Arab women, we have to learn from you—but I think it is a mutual relationship, where we both can learn from each other. I always say that you learn to know yourself better once you meet the other.

What I wish for is a face-to-face encounter between women. That would help them realize who they are and who the other is. Women are so creative and can think of so many things they can do then. I think in that sense, what I wish for is that American women, when they hear "Palestine," have a name, a face, and a story to connect to.

Reprinted by permission from *Lutheran Woman Today*, January-February 2002.

— Those Who Have Ears to Hear May Hear —

In March 2001, Viola Raheb wrote the following diary meditation on the Israeli military actions in Bethlehem's largest refugee camp. She discusses how we understand violence, the international media's coverage of the situation, and the need for "ears to hear."

Palestinian diary

The day is Monday, March 11, 2002. It is 6 P.M. in the evening and I have just returned home from the International Center, where we have been trying to overcome our sense of helplessness in the midst of all the agony surrounding us. Throughout the day, we have been busy sending reports and e-mails to people all over the world on the situation here in Bethlehem. At a time when the world seems to be deaf to our cry, we write hoping that those who have ears to hear will eventually hear

I sit in front of the TV to watch the international evening news. Yet, the local TV in Bethlehem is broadcasting pictures of the day. I decide to watch this coverage instead. The location of the report being broadcast is the Deheisha refugee camp, the largest refugee camp in the Bethlehem area, with almost 12,000 inhabitants. On the screen there are pictures of the Israeli military forcing children and men between the ages of 14-50, all civilians, to gather in a nearby open yard. Hundreds of children and men stand in the yard on a hot summer-like day, with temperature around 28° C (88° F). Soldiers are asking the assembled men and children to stand in rows, five to six men across. A row is called and that row of children and men are asked to take off the clothes from their upper body and put them in a plastic bag, which they then are asked to carry.

Following this, the soldiers investigate the men's ID cards, which seem to decide who are the chosen or the un-chosen ones. While the "un-chosen" are referred to the side, the chosen are taken, their hands tied, their eyes blindfolded before they are forced to enter the closed compound of a factory in the area. The scenes seem as if they are from a Hollywood horror movie. But this is no movie. These actions led to 600 detainees from Deheisha that day. A journalist asks one of the detainees, "Why are you not resisting?" The young man answers, "What is left to resist when you are being harassed by armed soldiers, while your hands are bound and your eyes blindfolded?"

Hearing the words of the young man from Deheisha made me think of a poem written by the Jewish poet Erich Fried entitled "Violence." The poem goes like this:

Violence is there where the State is saying:

In order to fight violence there can be no violence but mine.

Violence is there where you are told you are allowed to use
  violence and . . . where you are told you are not allowed to use it . . .

The constitution of violence states: what we do that is right
  and what the others do that is violence.

Violence may not be overcome by violence
  but maybe also not always without violence."

(English translation by Viola Raheb of the German poem in Erich Fried, "Voruebung fuer ein Wunder—Gedichte vom Zorn und Von der Liebe" Wagenbachs Taschenbuch, 1999, 356.)

In spite of the fact that these lines were written some time ago in another country by a Jew, I cannot help but see them reflected in what is happening to the men of Deheisha, standing in line surrounded by the Israeli military. Yes, at a time when the Israeli Army is invading Palestinian towns, villages, and refugee camps, the Sharon government seems to have as its watchword, "In order to fight violence there can be no violence but mine." And the world seems to buy this argument. But what else can we expect of a world so thirsty and thrilled to fight "terror"?!

Yet, with all these ideas in my mind, I could not help but think of the strong symbol of nonviolent resistance set by the people of Deheisha just a few days ago. While anticipating the Israeli invasion to their refugee camp, the people of Deheisha and their institutions wrote a press release, in which they declared that they are unarmed civilians who just want to live, who are carrying no weapons, and who are sure not going to use any [weapons]. This extraordinary decision of the people of Deheisha refugee camp turned the coin upside down. The Israeli army may have the military power over us, but they do not have the power over our decisions and morale.

Later that evening I sat down to hear the international news. Somehow I was not surprised that Deheisha's side of the story did not make it into the news. I could not help but think of another line by Erich Fried, "Violence is there where it imprisons its adversary, stigmatizing them as the origin of violence."

Viola Raheb

Questions for reflection and discussion

1. Viola Raheb describes daily life under occupation: its affect on her ability to move from one place to another, to get medical care, to go to work, even to sleep at night. Will there be water, electricity, or phone? What do you imagine it would be like to live in this way?

2. Two nations—two peoples—existing next to each other. Viola Raheb thinks the solution to the crisis is not about loving one another; it's about my accepting you even if I cannot love you. What do you think? In what ways is accepting one another enough (or not enough)?

3. How often do you see or hear the point of view of Palestinians in the media? What would responsible media coverage of occupation look like?

3

Pastor Mary Jensen

The Rev. Mary E. Jensen is a pastor of the ELCA, working in Jerusalem through the Division for Global Mission. She serves the Evangelical Lutheran Church in Jerusalem as communications assistant to Bishop Munib Younan.

⏤ Names and Connections ⏤

Pastor Jensen sends regular reports and reflections to her former congregation at Canyon Country, California and to a cadre of ELCA members concerned about peace in Israel and Palestine. Writing from Jerusalem on November 25, 2002, she uses an explanation of Arab practice concerning family names to describe the close connectedness of Palestinian families and the ways that closeness is disrupted by the occupation.

Greetings from Jerusalem where the rains of winter have begun to fall. The month of Ramadan for our Muslim friends began on November 6. Observant Muslims are fasting from dawn to dusk each day, and then enjoying their literal "break-fast" meal together as families and friends each evening. Ramadan is over about December 4 or 5, and then the Eid is celebrated. This is a festive holiday time of several days: gifts are exchanged, schools are closed, as are many businesses.

I want to explain two Arabic words, *Abu* and *Im* (pronounced AH-boo and IHM), which respectively mean "father" and "mother." We are in the season of family gatherings, and these words are very common. I hear them and use them every day.

First let me describe a custom among Arab Palestinian people regarding names. Everyone has at least one given name, and also the family name, just as most of us do. In addition, when a man or woman first becomes the parent of a son, the person is lovingly given another name, used among family and friends. This name reflects the relationship of father or mother and the firstborn son. For example, a man whose given name is Marwan may have a firstborn son who is named Yacub. Once the son is born, Marwan becomes Abu Yacub. The boy's mother is known as Im Yacub. The names mean "father of Yacub" and "mother of Yacub."

The parents still retain their legal names, of course, but for the rest of their lives they are known as the father and mother of Yacub. What happens if a girl is born first? Arab society is still very patriarchal so the firstborn son receives this honor, but I have known some fathers and mothers who are happy to be called Abu Marta or Im Marta, for instance, if the firstborn child is a girl named Marta. However, if the second or fifth or eighth baby is a boy, named Yacub, for example, then the parents become Abu and Im Yacub. If there are no boys in the family, only girls, then the parents may use the name of the oldest daughter, or in some cases the man may take the name of his father.

Unmarried men take the name of their father so they, too, may have the family designation of Abu. It is simply assumed that the unmarried man or the childless married man, if he ever has a son, will name his firstborn son after the father so the name is given in advance, even if there never is a firstborn son. To be Abu and Im is very, very special and important in Arab society. I've been asked the name of my firstborn son, and once in awhile I am called Im Dan.

There's another common custom regarding the naming of the firstborn son. It often happens in a family that two male names are used alternately generation after generation. So to use the example above, the father Marwan names his firstborn son Yacub. Why? Probably because Marwan's father was Yacub, and his grandfather was Marwan, and his great-grandfather was Yacub. When the son Yacub marries and has his firstborn son, the boy will be named

Marwan and that boy's son will be named Yacub. I have also heard of some families where the firstborn son actually gets both names, but in reverse order from his father. For example, Marwan Yacub will name his son Yacub Marwan and he, in turn, will name his firstborn son Marwan Yacub. I have one friend whose name is Yacub Mousa Mousa, the family name being Mousa. His father's name was Mousa Yacub Mousa.

The names connect the generations of the family to one another in a very common, specific, and tangible way. Within communities, people will automatically know who belongs to who, what family or father or son or mother is being addressed. A firstborn son is connected to his father and his father's father and to his son and his son's son forever by all their names. Other children in the family will probably receive family names, too. Sometimes there is a variation and a different name is used, unusual to the family. Chances are, however, that that name will be carried into future generations.

Families and clans are very connected in Arab society. The tradition is to live near one's family so many relatives are very close by. Palestinian villages I have visited are often populated by extended families so that nearly everyone is related. In towns or villages it often happens that the married sons in a family will either live with the parents or will build one or more flats on top of the family home. The daughters go to live with their husbands' families when they marry, perhaps in extra floors built on the husbands' family homes. New houses may be built, of course, or flats can be rented nearby, but in any case the extended family remains very close.

For Palestinian families there have been many disruptions because of the Israeli/Palestinian conflict and the Israeli military occupation.

1) Many Palestinians, both Christians and Muslims, are emigrating from Palestine in order to find a better life for their children or to find work. In some cases there is forced deportation by the Israeli military authority. This means that parents and grown children are

separated from one another by thousands of kilometers and by vast oceans. American families may be accustomed to living far from their parents and children, but Palestinian families are not. It is a very painful experience and leaves people feeling empty, abandoned, and depressed. It is very sad to note that the Christian Palestinian population is diminishing drastically in Palestine because of emigration. Today probably two percent or less of the Palestinian population is Christian. This, in turn, puts tremendous pressure on Christian churches and institutions to help maintain Christian identity, community, and cohesiveness for the Christian Palestinians who remain.

2) Even when members of a family remain in this land, they can be separated by artificial boundaries created by the Israeli military authority. For example, I know a woman from Beit Sahour in the Bethlehem area who is married to a man from Jerusalem. When they were married she moved to Jerusalem to be with her husband and his family, but she has been denied a permanent Jerusalemite identity card from the Israeli government. She must use her West Bank ID, which means she must get a special permit to be in Jerusalem.

She has now been without this special permit for nearly a year because of delays and strikes, and she must constantly be alert to avoid situations where she would have to show her ID. It has also been hard for her to find work in Jerusalem with her West Bank ID. Furthermore, she and her parents have a very difficult time seeing one another because the Bethlehem checkpoints are usually closed to Palestinians without special permits who want to enter Jerusalem and also because the woman has the ID problems herself.

The woman's parents had to travel many kilometers on back roads and through fields to attend the baptismal service of their grandchild in Jerusalem. And that was after the baptism had been postponed many times because of the Israeli military checkpoint barriers and because of lengthy curfews or lockdowns of the whole Bethlehem area. Similar situations affect almost every Palestinian family to one degree or another. Family life is disrupted and many kinds of problems arise.

In some places, such as the border between the Gaza Strip and Egypt, or between Syria and the Upper Galilee, Arab families can only see each other through fences, which are separated by many meters. They call to one another, shouting the news, holding up babies and children so they can be seen, inquiring about health and well-being. Many tears are shed at these barriers.

Currently Israel is building a high and very long wall between Israel and the West Bank area. The wall is being built on Palestinian land, thereby taking more land from Palestinians and separating more Palestinian towns and villages and families from one another.

3) Many young people are forced to wait to be married because of the lack of employment and also because of suitable housing. Traditionally the Palestinian man will provide housing, furniture, and lovely gifts for his bride. The housing ideally would be a new flat built on the man's parents' house, or a house right nearby. At least two problems can prevent this ideal situation:

a) The man is either unemployed or underemployed and cannot afford to live on his own, much less support a wife and family. If he is married, he brings his bride directly into his parents' household, and we all know the kinds of pressures this arrangement can bring, despite family love and traditions. As many as four or five generations may be living together in one house.

b) The man may want to build another floor on his parents' house or build a nearby house, but depending on the location, he may need to apply for a building permit from the Israeli government. These permits are almost never granted.

Usually the man and his family will go ahead and build without the permit, but it is risky because sooner or later the Israeli government will probably take steps to destroy the building, stating it was illegally built and therefore must go. If the family lives in a Palestinian-administered area the building permit is usually easy to obtain, but the Palestinian Administration is becoming more and more disabled, leaving many Palestinian towns and villages without administration or protection.

As a result, many Palestinian young people are either waiting a long time to be married, or they do not marry at all. Or they move away and marry elsewhere. If they settle in another country, they are usually not allowed to move back to Palestine.

The disruption of family life and of personal relationships is very difficult, and contributes to the breakdown of Palestinian society. Actually, it is all part and parcel of the Israeli government's overall intention to "cleanse the land" of Palestinians. This cannot be done quickly, so the slow, painful process of separating families through laws and borders and barriers goes on. It is subtle, but very, very real.

Here are some biblical and theological reflections, remembering the importance of the Arab Palestinian relationship between father and firstborn son. You may or may not agree with my thoughts, and that's fine. But reflect with me for a few moments.

Jesus was Jewish by religion and Palestinian by nationality; he was Semitic, as are both Arabs and Jews today. This whole area was Palestine in Jesus' day, named by the Romans after the Philistines who lived here. Jesus was a master storyteller, a Semitic gift that we can see continuing right through the centuries to our own day. Many of Jesus' parables had to do with family, and particularly with fathers and sons.

Remember the parable of the loving father and the two sons? Or the little example of a man saying he needed to go home and bury his father before following Jesus, or another saying he must go home and say goodbye to his family? Or how a father would never feed his children stones and snakes, but bread and fish? These parables come right out of Palestinian village life, a culture that still survives today in many Arab Palestinian villages in the Galilee and the West Bank.

Biblically and theologically, we find Jesus speaking of his Father in heaven, and in John 3 we hear about Jesus being God's one and only Son. "Indeed, God did not send the Son into the world to condemn the world, but in order that the world might be saved through him" (John 3:17).

Where did this imagery of Father and Son come from? For the most part we simply accept it because it is in the Bible and in our theology. We don't think much about it, unless we get concerned about the patriarchal image, or we wonder how it is that we speak of Father, Son, and Holy Spirit, Three in One, One in Three. I certainly don't have all the answers to the mystery of the Trinity, but I finally do understand the Father-Son motif much better. In the culture and language in which both the Old and New Testaments were written, there was no closer relationship than that of father and firstborn son. They were nearly identical; they were as one. If the son spoke, it was like the father speaking.

If the father spoke, it was like the son speaking. The son had the authority of the father. Remember Jesus' parable about the bad tenants in the vineyard and the landowner who unsuccessfully sent servants and finally sent his son to collect the fruit. "They will respect my son," he said (see Matthew 21:37). Why? Because sending the son was like coming himself. But the tenants killed the son instead, rejecting both father and son.

No wonder our Savior spoke so lovingly of his Father in heaven. No wonder that the human, cultural experience of father and firstborn son was used to express the relationship between God the Father and Jesus the Son, between the Creator and the Redeemer. For me, it is using human, cultural language to say that Jesus, born into the tribe of David in the little town of Bethlehem, was God incarnate, God in human flesh, Emmanuel, God with us. No longer does it puzzle me to think of God as Father and Jesus as God's one and only Son, because I know that it means they are one and the same, even as in a very human way I see the father and firstborn son relationships in Palestinian society today.

One more thing. In Luke 8 we hear about Jesus' mother and brothers who came to see him while he was teaching a crowd of people. When told that his mother and brothers were standing outside, Jesus said, "My mother and my brothers are those who hear the word of God and do it" (Luke 8:21). Knowing how important family was and is in this culture, it is incredibly telling and so beautiful to know that Jesus opens his arms to envelope everyone who hears and obeys God's Word into his family.

Mary E. Jensen, also known as Im Dan.

~ A Visit to Aboud—May 2002 ~

Pastor Mary Jensen and a medical team from the Lutheran Augusta Victoria Hospital encountered blockades and checkpoints on their way to the town of Aboud. Once there, they received a beautiful welcome and were taken to see an ancient Christian church and a sacred shrine precious to the town's heritage.

Aboud (pronounced ah-BOOD) is a lovely town of about 2,000 Christian and Muslim Palestinian people located in the West Bank, northwest of Ramallah. There are many small villages in this area, which is close to the western edge of the Israeli military Occupied Territories, as defined by the Green Line, an invisible border created after the 1967 war.

When driving to Aboud, the roadway is sometimes inside Israel, sometimes inside the West Bank, and is always patrolled by Israeli soldiers and vehicles—including tanks, jeeps, and armored personnel carriers (APCs). There are numerous military checkpoints where every vehicle traveling along the road must stop.

Aboud, like many other villages, has become isolated from the outside world in regard to travel into and out of the town. The usual roads have been dug up by Israeli bulldozers and are impassable. The only current entrance to Aboud is over a small hill on a dirt road, which leads between two houses and on to the main street of town. Many times this dirt road is impassable, blocked by an Israeli tank. Other times another entrance will be created, and then blocked. The citizens of Aboud are literally imprisoned in their own village. Some hardy folks will walk through fields and over hills to get out but it is dangerous business. They can be shot on sight by an Israeli sniper. But what if there's a medical emergency? What if there is need to visit family outside the village or obtain emergency supplies or legal papers? People either suffer through the circumstances or take incredible chances to make the strenuous walk through rocky, rough, hilly terrain. This scenario is repeated in scores of villages in the West Bank.

The Lutheran World Federation (LWF) through Augusta Victoria Hospital on the Mount of Olives in Jerusalem provides village health clinics in the West Bank. Aboud is one of the towns that receive medical service from Augusta Victoria. The town has provided a small clinic for the doctor and nurses to use when they come. Usually the visits to Aboud are scheduled twice a week but the specially-marked medical vans are often turned back at the various Israeli checkpoints, making it impossible to enter Aboud and see patients on any kind of regular schedule.

On Friday, May 17, 2002, I was fortunate to visit Aboud. I traveled in the Augusta Victoria medical van with Dr. Osama, several nurses, and two other ELCA pastors, including my brother, the Rev. John Halvorson, Director of the ELCA World Hunger Program, and the Rev. Franklin Ishida, Division for Global Mission (DGM) Director for International Scholarships and International Communications. Each time we approached an Israeli checkpoint the doctor would become tense, hoping this time the van would be allowed to pass. We were stopped several times, our passports were checked, we waited for Israeli soldiers to check our papers and the vehicle, but fortunately we were allowed to pass each checkpoint this day. The doctor was ecstatic!

There was one more potential problem before we could actually enter Aboud. The big question was: Would an Israeli tank be blocking the dirt road at the top of the hill right outside Aboud? Usually the tank was hidden from sight until the last moment, so everyone in the medical van waited until they saw no tank was waiting behind the dirt mound and then gave a collective shout of joy. Aboud would receive medical care today!

The main road of Aboud has many lovely homes and trees. The gorgeous red and violet bougainvillea was spilling over walls and climbing up trees. The medical van was parked by the small, neat clinic and the doors were opened for business. A few people filtered in, very surprised and pleased to see the doctor and nurses.

In the meantime our little group of ELCA pastors plus a Danish nurse, Ruth, began wandering along the main street of Aboud, greeting people and taking pictures. One man named Jamal (whose English was at about the same level as my Arabic) offered to show us "the old church." We knew the Christian mayor (*mukhtar*) of Aboud was coming to give us a tour of the town, so we asked Jamal to wait a few moments. And sure enough—here came the mayor, Ilias Aazar, driving his car. By this time another Christian man named Hani had also arrived and because he spoke much better English than Jamal, we had ourselves a tour guide. We opted to walk to the old church and the mayor would meet us there in his car.

So off we went—Jamal and Hani in the lead, and the rest of us, American and Danish, following after them. They showed us the Caritas Clinic, one more source of medical care, thank God! We passed by the Latin Catholic Church, very nice, with a lovely grotto, and continued up the gentle hill to the very old Greek Orthodox Church. Along the way we found signs painted on the neat walls—not graffiti but meaningful symbols, Christian symbols. Hani told us the young people had painted the walls during the Christmas season and the crosses and greetings were still very bright in May. The village is about half Christian, half Muslim, and everyone is a neighbor to the other.

When these people said "old," they meant *Oollllddd*! This church is said to have been built in the fourth century A.D. and there are many archeological indications that this is true, including a stone inscription of dedication in what appears to be the Aramaic language, stating the event and the year. With money from the Palestinian Authority, the town has been able to do work uncovering the ancient walls and columns that have been hidden for centuries underneath plaster and paint. An ancient mosaic floor was uncovered outside the present church building, and a very old entrance into the church is visible at a much lower level than the current street.

Once inside the church, which houses a worshiping community in Aboud, we had to go down several steps to the main floor. The church had been built almost in a square, with the iconostasis at the front and many icons on and behind the screen and also in the congregational part of the church. There was one large icon hanging on a column that portrayed John the Baptist holding a large chalice, offering it to the viewer. Inside the chalice was a tiny but complete portrayal of the crucified and risen Christ. This was an icon I had never before seen in any church or book or collection of icons. The viewer was being offered Christ in the Sacrament of Holy Communion. I found it quite amazing and quite beautiful.

Mayor Ilias and Hani were anxious to show us the work that had been done, taking off centuries of plaster and paint to show the original fourth-century walls and columns. Stories and legends abound in regard to events and miracles that have happened in this church. One story tells about a time of war, many centuries ago, when a Muslim man from the village rushed to the church for safety. He pounded on the church door, begging that his life be spared. From inside, the story goes, the man heard a voice saying he would be safe. As a gift of thanksgiving, he brought a supply of oil to the church every year. Hani told us that the man's descendants still bring oil to this church, remembering the miracle of safety at the door.

The mayor then invited us to his home for coffee. He led us slowly along some streets to his house. On the way we said hello to people, received little gifts of flowers and fresh chickpeas. I could hear sheep and lambs making their baaing noises, and was surprised and delighted to find the herd of sheep in their pen, which was the ground floor underneath the owner's house. The father and son of the family were inside, caring for the animals. I couldn't resist—I took pictures of those sheep! I got one close-up picture of a sheep staring at me, which just cracks me up!

Soon we arrived at the mayor's house, climbing up outside steps and walking into a lovely enclosed verandah. There were beautiful views of the rolling hills around Aboud. We sat comfortably, drinking juice and coffee, visiting and enjoying the view. It was impossible to tell at that moment that the people and the village were actually prisoners of the Israeli military, experiencing unemployment, health, family, and emotional problems due to the closures. Rather, it was a lovely spring day in Aboud.

When I started asking questions about old photographs on the wall, we learned about the mayor's father who had built this house in 1934 while he was still living in Jaffa, right on the Mediterranean Sea, near modern day Tel Aviv. This village was like a vacation spot for the family; they enjoyed both homes.

It was about then that we started hearing women calling to us from the next room. "Why don't you come and see us?" they said. Curious, and dismayed that I hadn't realized the women were so nearby, I went into the adjoining room and found three women of the family busy making a special meat pastry, called *ikbab*. It is a special food enjoyed by the Christians in Aboud after Easter each year. I sat down with the women to see how they made the delicacy and soon was joined by Ruth, Franklin, and John. We all got to taste the delicious meat pastry being made by the mayor's wife and his sister and mother.

We were invited to see how the balls of meat and dough were being boiled in a cooker, so we followed the sister into the kitchen, then through a narrow doorway into a bedroom. Here we saw a vat filled with boiling water, into which the mayor's wife was carefully placing the dough balls, which were lined up on a towel on the floor. As we returned to the main room, the women showed us the tiny "Jaffa tiles" that were laid on all the floors. These were very old, colorful tiles, with damage in only a few places. Undoubtedly they were original with the house.

Only too soon it was time to leave the mayor's house and return to the clinic where the doctor and nurses were probably finishing their work. Right next to the mayor's house was the mosque, and since it was a Friday many Muslim people were gathered to pray.

Walking past the old church and back down the hill, our tour guides pointed out another hill in the distance, marked at the top by green trees and a small building over a cave. We were told this was a shrine to Saint Barbara and was very holy and special to all the people of Aboud. Various prayers and activities were held at the shrine, we were told, especially on Saint Barbara's Day. Like the old church, this shrine was very, very old, dating back many centuries, and had many stories and beliefs connected to it. It was a sacred place.

The Muslim prayers were ending as we climbed back into the medical van and began driving out of Aboud. Suddenly we noticed that the village calm was shaken when several jeeps carrying Israeli soldiers drove into Aboud and began cruising around. In many ways it did seem to be an incitement to unrest in a village that had been going about its own business on an ordinary Friday.

The calmness and ordinariness of Aboud are rather deceiving, sad to say. Oh, the village is lovely and one of my favorites, and I know at least one person in the United States who is from Aboud and confirms my impression of a fine village. But the Israeli military occupation and its arbitrary harshness are felt at every level of village life. Closing in the occupants by destroying roads and prohibiting travel takes work, commerce, medical care, business dealings, and social gatherings away from the people—in other words, it breaks down the society. Is this the reason for imposing such hardships? Is it Israel's intention to be sure that Palestinian village life wastes away? Young people will undoubtedly leave the villages. Land confiscation makes farming impossible. In a matter of years only elderly people will remain, and when they die, so will Aboud.

A part of Aboud died suddenly at 9 P.M. on Friday, May 31, 2002, just two weeks after I had visited with the people, took a funny photo of a sheep, and ate *ikbab* at the mayor's house. The villagers had been watching a lot of Israeli military activity for several hours on the hill where Saint Barbara's shrine was located. They stood in the village streets and in the fields, dreading what was happening in the holy place. Then, right at 9 P.M., the soldiers destroyed the cave and little building with explosives. I can only imagine how the people must have cried out and wept. My U.S. friend from Aboud says that the shrine was "the soul of the village." A few days later the villagers gathered on the hill to pray and to mourn the loss of their shrine, sacred to the villagers for so many centuries.

What was the point of destroying the Saint Barbara shrine? To damage Christianity in the village? To drive home the point that Israel is in control of Aboud? Or is it just the beginning of more Israeli activity on the lovely hill? Will a new illegal Israeli settlement be built on Aboud's land? Only time will tell.

I hope you, too, can perhaps feel the life and love of this village named Aboud, and then tell the story of the Israeli military's treatment of people in Aboud and many other villages, people who simply want to live their traditional lives in the freedom of a Palestinian state, free of the Israeli military occupation.

Questions for reflection and discussion

1. Separation of families is painful in any culture. In the United States, family members are fairly comfortable living hundreds of miles from one another. In what ways do you relate to the frustration and grief of close-knit families being pulled apart?

2. Pastor Mary Jensen refers briefly to the parable of the loving father with two sons. Do you recognize it as the story we call the prodigal son? How does this story relate to Pastor Jensen's discussion of family in Palestine?

3. What naming traditions does your family have?

4. Hospitality plays an important role in Palestinian culture. Have you ever encountered a welcome like the one Pastor Mary Jensen and her group found at Aboud? Share what happened. What actions showed welcome to you?

5. The people of Aboud were glad to have visitors and proud to show them around town. It feels good to share our town with foreigners, to tour them around our most precious places. In what ways does your church show welcome to strangers and outsiders?

4

Dr. Nuha Khoury

Dr. Nuha Khoury, a native of Bethlehem, returned to Palestine in 1996 after studying at the University of Michigan. She serves as the Deputy Director of the Dar al-Kalima Model School and Academy project of the International Center of Bethlehem.

⌐ Wholesale Imprisonment ⌐

In this message to friends of the International Center in November 2000, Dr. Khoury provides background to the military "closure" or shutdown of cities in the West Bank and Gaza and describes the implications of a violent occupation. It would be a year before the first Israeli incursion into Bethlehem.

Bethlehem, the besieged city, has been silenced by the international media. Over the past few years, we Palestinians have exerted all efforts possible in the peace negotiations, hoping that they will lead the region to peace and prosperity. Yet, since the Madrid talks and after ten years of negotiations, the situation has not improved for Palestinians, but rather has been deteriorating rapidly. The visit of (Ariel) Sharon to the Al-Aqsa Mosque was the last straw that brought to the surface the frustration and disillusionment of the Palestinian people who for the last ten years were anxiously waiting for peace to bear fruits. The brutal response of Israel to the Palestinians' peaceful demonstrations helped to escalate the situation even further.

In the last two weeks, the reaction of Israel to Palestinian demonstrators has taken on new dimensions. On the one hand Israel is not only using live ammunition but also bombing Palestinian city centers with tanks and Apache helicopters. Yesterday, October 12, the bombing escalated when Israel bombarded the main centers of the Palestinian National Authority in Gaza City, Ramallah, and Jericho.

Moreover, in the last few weeks we are in a situation where not only are we attacked by the Israeli army but also by Jewish Israeli settlers. These settlers are trigger-happy and have been organizing night attacks on unarmed civilians while being protected by the Israeli army. Not only are these settlers attacking us Palestinians in the Occupied Territories, but they are also attacking the Palestinian Arabs in Israel, who are Israeli citizens.

As a result of the attacks by the army and settlers on the Palestinians more than 107 Palestinians are dead and more than 3,750 injured. Among those injured, a large number will be permanently handicapped. The tragedy of the situation is not only the use of heavy weapons against us, but also the siege under which we live. For the past two weeks, the Palestinian Autonomous areas, which makes up 3 percent of the land area of the West Bank, is totally closed off. Our freedom of movement is limited to a two-kilometer radius. As a direct result of the siege, we are suffering a shortage of food supplies and most importantly of medical supplies. In addition, Israel has cut off electricity as well as water supplies in many Palestinian areas, especially in Gaza. Therefore, we are now fighting for both our safety and daily survival.

At the International Center of Bethlehem, whose work revolves around the local community, we are mainly worried about the young children, who constitute up to 60 percent of our population. They are traumatized by the experience and are constantly worried for their safety and that of their parents. Many of them are having nightmares, which has led some organizations to establish hotlines offering counseling for them and their parents. The image of Muhammad, the 12-year-old boy who was killed execution style by the Israeli soldiers, is haunting both Palestinian children and parents, who watched the helplessness of Muhammad's father and his inability to protect his son from the Israeli bullets that killed the son and left the father permanently paralyzed.

In the midst of all our sorrow and pain we feel that we are being forgotten by the world community. However, we thank God for all the friends who have been continuously calling us and sending us messages of support. It gives us hope to know that while we are silenced, there are those who are articulating our voice and lifting up our worries in front of God. We would like to take this opportunity to ask you to continue to keep us in your thoughts and prayers and to continue your struggle for a just peace for all God's children.

◦ To the Young People on the Other Side ◦

Dr. Nuha Khoury, Deputy Director of the Dar al-Kalima Model School and Academy project of the International Center of Bethlehem, facilitated the creation of this letter from the Palestinian children to Israeli youth.

An Open Letter From the Children of Dar al-Kalima Academy

Last Friday, as some of your peers were waiting to be admitted to a discotheque in Tel Aviv, we were busy putting the final touches for the inauguration ceremony of our new school, the Dar al-Kalima Academy. Some of us were rehearsing the play that explained the strategy of our model school, which promotes critical thinking, creativity, and communications. Others were busy decorating the classrooms with displays of their work. Many were hanging the colorful banners on the stage. For a whole year we waited and worked very hard for this opening. Friends of ours came especially from the United States and Norway to celebrate with us. Our excitement was boundless. We wanted our parents and friends to see our school the way we see it, a model school full of promise and joy as well as a place through which we can shape a better future for ourselves.

Exhausted, we went home to sleep, dreaming about the inauguration when we could sing and dance in celebration. Yet, our festivities never materialized. We woke up to the news that children, almost our age, were killed as a result of a suicide bombing by another young person. Although you are the children on the Other Side, and although your parents might be actively involved in maintaining the occupation of our land, we want you to know that we grieved for the loss of so many young lives. We felt that our celebration will not be as joyful as we had hoped it would be. We went to the school on Saturday morning to do the final rehearsals. We were rehearsing our school anthem, which we wrote to express our school's philosophy, calling for dialogue not violence, peaceful coexistence with our neighbors rather than conflict and occupation.

In the final moments of preparations, the decision was made to cancel the ceremony. We could not believe that all of our work for the past year was in vain and that the whole momentum that was building up will be lost. We tried to object, but many people were afraid that Prime Minister Ariel Sharon would take revenge and strike our cities and villages, even bombard our school, with F-16 planes. All roads leading to Bethlehem were closed and only then we realized that all the guests whom we invited would not make it. We went home with heavy hearts and waited in fear: What if they really strike our beautiful school? Where would we play soccer and basketball? What if our new Millenium Stage becomes only a heap of steel? What if the small trees we planted and tended with love and care will be burnt and the birds' nests on top of the old trees were destroyed causing the birds to migrate?

Although you live just on the other side of the fence, we wonder how much you really know about our situation. Did you hear, for example, that even the school group that was planning to travel to Germany this week to represent us was denied travel by the Israeli government? Do you know what it means to be denied movement and that all your plans depend on the "grace" of the Israeli military?

We wonder why only a few are taking note of our ongoing suffering for the past 34 years. Why is it that not many people are grieving for our lost childhood? We ask ourselves constantly if one people can have a monopoly over suffering or if there are children whose suffering is less significant than other children's suffering.

We ask ourselves every day if it is our joint destiny to continue being the victims of this ongoing conflict. We ask ourselves how many more generations of children on both sides have to continue to worry about their future and suffer endlessly? Is it not the time for you and for us to raise our voices and to work hand-in-hand for justice, peace, and coexistence? We believe that conflict is not and should not be our fate. So, let us commit ourselves to challenge our present so that our future and that of our children will be promising. It takes very little to wage war, but building peace requires a continuous, tremendous, and endless commitment. We can either continue to live in the hell of the present or strive toward living life in dignity. The choice is ours to make.

Questions for reflection and discussion

1. Dr. Nuha Khoury wrote, "In the midst of all our sorrow and pain we feel that we are being forgotten by the world community." Do you think she is right? What evidence supports or rejects her position?

2. Fear of the settlers is a factor in Nuha Khoury's message. Israeli settlers are a varied lot—some fundamentalists, some violent, many others average folks who have found an affordable apartment. Settlements are highly-developed housing complexes, with parks, soccer fields, convenience stores, and their own "bypass" roads that Palestinians may not drive on. Almost always this is on land confiscated from the original Palestinian owners and surrounded by military buffer zones. What would it be like to go harvest in your fields or orchards and have to anticipate encountering soldiers or armed settlers?

3. Why do you think Dr Khoury's students feel invisible to the Israeli youth only a few miles away in Israel? Do you think Dr. Khoury's students are invisible to our U.S. youth and adults? What kind of letter would high school kids in the United States write to the Palestinian children?

4. What would it be like if youth from Israel could visit the Dar al-Kalima school? What might it be like if the children of Bethlehem could make a trip to Israel? Youth from Palestine will join ELCA teens at the youth gathering in 2003. What questions might that encounter raise for ELCA young people?

5

Pastor Mitri Raheb

The Rev. Mitri Raheb is the pastor of Evangelical Christmas Lutheran Church in Bethlehem, in the occupied West Bank. A native of Bethlehem, he is the founder of the International Center of Bethlehem and the Dar al-Kalima Model School and Academy.

⏤ Mr. Clinton, What Would You Do If You Were in My Shoes? ⏤

In January 2001 Pastor Raheb sent this letter to President Bill Clinton and published it on the Web site of the International Center of Bethlehem. It describes the oppressive experience of roadblocks and checkpoints that deny Palestinian people any free movement. This treatment deprives the Palestinian people of human dignity.

Mr. President, allow me first to introduce myself to you. I am a Palestinian Christian, born and raised in Bethlehem, and the pastor of Christmas Lutheran Church as well as the director of the International Center of Bethlehem. We met two years ago here in Bethlehem, and you may have read my book *Bethlehem 2000*, presented to you by President Arafat on the occasion of your visit. Today, I was supposed to arrive to your country together with my wife, who happens to hold a U.S. green card. We were invited by friends and fellow Christians from Florida, Illinois, Kansas, and Missouri, who were anticipating our visit as much as we were. They worked very hard for the past three months to organize for me a series of lectures, preaching engagements, and important meetings. However, I find myself sitting in my office in Bethlehem today writing you this letter instead.

I know of your commitment to peace in this region. I read your recent proposals, as released. At first, I thought that they were interesting. Then, a second reading showed me how vague they were. But after my experience yesterday, I found that they do not contain the promise of freedom, peace, and dignity that they claim.

Let me start by asking you a simple question. What would it take for an average American to travel abroad, besides a valid passport, a visa, and a ticket? Not much more, I would say. Yet for a Palestinian, travel is a totally different story. A Palestinian cannot leave the country without a travel permit. For me, living in Bethlehem, these permits are issued by the Israeli military based in the illegally built settlement bloc by the name of Gosh Ezion, located six miles south of Bethlehem.

Yet how can one reach Gosh Ezion if Bethlehem is sealed off and, in a Palestinian green-license-plate car, one is allowed to drive in a one-mile radius only? First, I had to get a yellow-license-plate taxi to travel on one of the so called bypass roads, built on confiscated Palestinian land yet designed mainly for the use of Israeli settlers. I met the taxi on December 28 at one of the many roadblocks that the Israelis have placed to divide the Bethlehem districts into pieces. Once we reached our destination my wife and I submitted our applications, and we were told that it is forbidden for Palestinians to leave the country except if they possess foreign passports. We were instructed to come back in three days to see if we can get these permits.

On December 31, I called the Israeli military authority to inquire if we were granted the permits and was told that my wife did, but I was denied. The reason given was that my wife has a green card and I do not. I told them that as a clergyman I have a Vatican passport. The soldier said, "Then, you should fill new forms, attach a copy of your passport and apply again." I did as told.

We drove again to the roadblock to catch a yellow-license-plate taxi and found that there was a small opening in the road that would allow my car through. I decided to take the chance and I drove my own car heading to the settlement. During this six-mile journey my wife and I were most afraid of what might happen to us if a settler decided that our presence on the road was not to his or her liking. Finally, we reached our destination and got our permits.

We returned to the roadblock and tried to get in the way we went out, but an Israeli military vehicle was standing there. He pointed the gun at us and told us to go back to the place we came from. I told my wife not to worry, that we would go to other roadblocks to see if there were any openings. It was then that we started our *Via Dolorosa* (the way of suffering/the cross), traveling from one road-block to another. For more than one hour we kept trying, and I kept thinking about how villagers commuting to the town every day suffer as a result of Bethlehem being sealed off. Finally, we found an opening in one of the roadblocks and were able to enter our Little Town of Bethlehem before the soldiers saw us and closed the opening.

Yesterday, on January 4, we started at 9:30 A.M., in a yellow-license-plate car, for Ben Gurion airport, which is about 30 miles northwest of Bethlehem, to catch our 4:35 P.M. flight. The soldiers at the entrance of Bethlehem stopped the car, asked for the permits, checked them and allowed us to go through. We arrived at the airport early and were the first in line.

We handed our passports, tickets, and permits to the security official, who looked at the permit and then at us and at the permits again. She told us that our permits are not valid and that we cannot fly. "But, the people who issued them reassured me yesterday on the phone that they are," I argued. She said that she would check with the airport police, who told her that the permits were invalid.

Prepared for anything, I had the phone number of the military authorities who issued the permits and I called them. I spoke to the captain, who reassured me that the permits are valid. I gave my cellular phone to the security officer to hear it for herself. She sent another officer to the airport police, who returned with the answer, "NO PALESTINIAN IS ALLOWED TO LEAVE THE COUNTRY."

"Let me talk to the police authorities myself," I said.

"You should look for them yourself, try the information desk," was her answer. In the meantime her boss came and shouted at her for wasting time talking to us. She left and I started my search for the police, leaving my wife at the counter with the luggage. I was prohibited to get to the airport police, which one can only reach if one has the boarding pass. Finally, I was told to walk to the police headquarters, which is located outside the main building of the airport. Once I got there, they wouldn't let me in. The woman at the desk dialed a number and handed me the phone.

I explained to the policewoman on the other end what was going on, and her answer was, "NO PALESTINIAN IS ALLOWED TO LEAVE THE COUNTRY. These are our instructions." She refused to take the number of the military authorities to talk to them and insisted that they should talk to her. I called the military authorities again and asked them to talk to the airport police. He promised to do so. And for the next three hours our *Via Dolorosa* continued between the military authorities, airport police, and airport security. At 3:35 P.M. I called the captain at Gosh Ezion who told me that he tried his best, but that there are orders which he cannot overrule and so we cannot travel today, but that I should wait until things calm down.

I asked myself, how can things calm down if they continue treating people like that? What would you do, Mr. President, if you were in my shoes? I am not talking about the financial loss from the taxis and flight tickets. Neither am I talking about lost time and stress. Rather, I am talking about basic human rights of free movement and of living in dignity. What would you do if you were in my shoes?

Many Palestinians, especially Christians, choose the option of emigration. They leave to live in the Promised Land of the U.S.A., thus emptying the Promised Land of Palestine of its resources, potential, and promise. Others are radicalized by such treatment. The constant inhuman treatment eliminates their imagination of a better life here and now. If you are treated like they are treated, Mr. President, I am sure you will not act differently. But you are never treated like that. In two weeks you will leave office, with or without an agreement. But we Palestinians are here to stay. For better or for worse, we have to live with whichever agreement is brokered by your country.

Here, I ask myself, what would I, Mitri Raheb, do if I were in your shoes? If I were in your shoes, I would make sure that the Palestinians will have real sovereignty, and control over their borders, their bypass-free roads, and their airspace, so that tomorrow not one single Palestinian would be treated the way I was treated yesterday. I am not talking about luxury, but rather about living without humiliation. If I were in your shoes, I would follow the footprints of Christ and do everything possible to bring justice, healing, and hope to the land in which 2,000 years ago the Divine gave humanity its new meaning, dignity, and promise.

The Rev. Mitri Raheb
Christmas Lutheran Church
Bethlehem

~ Giving the Children of Bethlehem Future and Hope: The Story of the Dar al-Kalima Model School ~

Education is a vital ministry of the Evangelical Lutheran Church in Jerusalem, sometimes described as "the heart of the church." More than half the people of Palestine are children and youth, so education is a priority. The Lutheran schools are committed to innovation, and Bethlehem's Dar al-Kalima School and Academy, the subject of Pastor Mitri Raheb's article, is an example. The congregations of the ELCJ also administer schools and other education programs in Ramallah, Beit Sahour, Beit Jala, and Jerusalem.

In the birthplace of Jesus, where the Word became a child, children are still at risk. Not only do they live in a quasi-war zone, they suffer from an outdated educational system that does not appreciate intellect, imprisons imagination, and crushes creativity.

As the father of two daughters, I experienced firsthand what this system did to our children. Together with many other parents, church members, and staff, we decided to start in Bethlehem a new model school, which we called "Dar al-Kalima," meaning "The House of the Word," the Word that chose to become flesh nowhere but in our little town.

It is always easy to dream of something new, but how to make this dream come true? Our vision seemed like a mission impossible. How can we start a new school, when we don't yet own the land where the school shall be built on, when we don't have the funds needed or the resources required? On faith, and faith alone, we started to look for a place. A dream place was Mount Murier, a distortion of the name Mueller. The Rev. Samuel Mueller, the first pastor for the Christmas Lutheran Church, was the one who bought the mountain in 1868 from its original owners. Yet this mountain was not at our disposal. The mountain was considered by the British Mandate as "German Enemy Property." In 1919, they confiscated it. Later, in the 1950s, the property was registered in the name of the "Treasury of the Hashemite Kingdom of Jordan" and thus lost forever.

These facts made the dream dissipate. Many people were telling me, "Do not waste your precious time on such a useless endeavor." Yet I was of the opinion that if God was able to give Abraham a child when he was 99 years old, then God can restore this land to its original owners—even after 80 years.

With the coming of the Palestinian National Authority and the support of the German Foreign Ministry, along with big efforts exerted by my colleagues at the International Center of Bethlehem, the dream came true. A six-and-a-half acre part of that beautiful mountain overlooking the Judean desert, the Dead Sea, Herodion, the Mount of Olives, and much more, was granted to us by President Arafat as a site for the Dar al-Kalima School.

One condition was put to us: We had to build the first phase of the school with within one year. When we broke ground in December 1999, we had about $70,000 U.S. dollars, less than 4 percent of the total cost.

On September 3, 2000, the school was fully in operation with more than 200 kids, a principal, and 33 teachers. We had still thousands of dollars in debts to the contractor, but God has been working to provide for us. Wheat Ridge Ministries, the ELCA, Lutheran churches from around the world, individuals, and foundations are coming together to give the children of Bethlehem future and hope. We are still far from the goal, yet we trust in no one else but in the Child of Bethlehem.

The Dar al-Kalima Model School is a Lutheran-based school serving the whole Palestinian community. The mission of the school is to offer quality education for all Palestinians, not only those who can afford it.

The school operates kindergarten through the tenth grade. An eleventh grade will be added in 2003. It is one of the few schools in the Bethlehem region that is coeducational and has a female enrollment of more than 40 percent. The student body reflects the social, economic, and religious diversity of the Palestinian community. Students come from different socioeconomic backgrounds (middle class, lower middle class, as well as poor and very needy families) and religious backgrounds (Muslims and Christians who are Lutheran, Orthodox, and Catholic), as well as residential areas (they come from the city, village, and refugee camps).

To enable all students to have access to the quality education that the school provides, the Lutheran church has taken upon itself a commitment to keep tuition fees reasonable and to provide a sponsorship program for the most economically disadvantaged.

Dar al-Kalima provides a positive model for other schools. Children's facilities to follow in that green space and open courtyards, essential for the development of healthy children, should be part of the architectural design. The school still lacks laboratories, library, administrative building, and teachers' facilities.

Dar al-Kalima's unique philosophy

Traditionally, the Palestinian school system has been based on rote learning and memorization. The Dar al-Kalima Model School was conceived with the idea to offer an alternative to the traditional system through a new educational concept that is based on a holistic approach to teaching. A philosophy consisting of seven 7 "Cs" was developed:

Christian values

The Middle East, even the whole world, is experiencing a crisis in terms of values. The increasing violence is but an expression of this crisis. The values, which Jesus taught, lived, and died for, are central in our education.

Child-oriented

The school actively works on changing the prevalent belief that the student is an observer in the educational process, an empty vessel that needs to be filled with knowledge by the teacher. Thus the Dar al-Kalima Model School aims at making the student an important and active participant in his or her educational process. Participatory learning lies at the heart of this approach.

Creativity

Palestine does not have many resources. To survive much creativity is needed. The school seeks to provide alternatives for our young people, who suffer from the lack of cultural programs in their school syllabus (such as music, drama, and art). These creative cultural programs are needed to help develop the personality of the students, but also to develop future leadership for the church and society.

Critical thinking

A system that is based on memorization and rote learning does not leave much room for creativity or critical thinking. Critical thinking is important as a base for any democracy. Democracy is important for the future of the Middle East and for the survival of Christianity in the region as well.

Communication

We see ourselves as part and parcel of a worldwide church, also of the one humanity. We want our children to be able to relate to and communicate with Christians from different countries and with people with diverse cultures.

Languages play an important role in our school. The main language at school is Arabic. We teach English starting in first grade and German starting in the third. French is offered as an additional option.

The computer lab is essential to connecting our children with many children in the world.

Commitment to the community

In the past centuries, all the bright students who got a good education ended up living outside of Palestine. Christians especially tended to emigrate more easily than Muslims. There is a real danger that the Holy Land would become a mere Christian Disneyland—a Christian theme park. Our school is committed to the children of Bethlehem so they then will commit themselves to serve their community.

Clubs and extracurricula activities

From the beginning the school started implementing the prolonged school day. The prolonged school day is based on the idea of having the students work in small groups or clubs on curricula and noncurricula subjects. Last year, the school offered 14 different clubs between Monday and Thursday of each week in the fields of art, music, ecology, handicrafts, languages, theater, science, cultural studies, and mathematics. The clubs' experience has shown that the students' performance has improved in general and that they have become more interested in what they are learning. Programs will be offered for parents as well, especially mothers, which will help them grow as individuals and will make of them active members in the life of the school.

We have ambitious goals

We seek to strengthen the Palestinian Christian identity and promote an active Palestinian Christian presence, witness, and outreach in the Holy Land. Our hope is to empower socially and economically marginalized families through offering their children equal educational opportunities. The schools will empower female students by integrating them in both academic and vocational training programs. We will promote the values of peace, democracy, coexistence, justice, and human rights in the Middle East.

Another goal is to strengthen the Palestinian educational infrastructure through offering a high quality and creative education. The school seeks to serve the local community through providing an innovative educational model that can be used by other schools in the area. We hope to nurture faith of students through responding to their different intellectual, emotional, and physical needs. Dar al-Kalima's intent is to discover and encourage the individual potentials, talents, abilities, and interests of the students. We look forward to promoting exchange programs between students, teachers, and educators of the school with others from the United States, Europe, Africa, and Asia.

This is how Dar al-Kalima was born. For it to grow, it needs the dedication and commitment of the administrators, the teachers, the students, and the parents. By faith and with the help of our Lord we were able to move mountains. What is much more difficult is changing minds, honing talents, releasing potentials, and convincing parents. Indeed, this is how Dar al-Kalima was born and built, but for it to grow and prosper it will need continuous prayers, support, and care. Our children are at risk and our society's future is at stake. We have much to do in Bethlehem, the place where the Word became a child.

Questions for reflection and discussion

1. How can things calm down in this part of the world if people keep humiliating one another, making travel and life impossible, and replacing dignity with fear?

2. If you were the president of the United States, how would you answer Pastor Raheb's letter?

3. What would you have done if you had been in Pastor Mitri Raheb's shoes?

4. Pastor Raheb's plans for Dar al-Kalima do not reveal, much less dwell on, the destruction the school experienced in the overwhelming Israeli military incursion of 2002. What do you imagine gives these people the hope and stamina it takes to rebuild and create a positive vision for the future?

5. In what ways are the Dar al-Kalima school's goals, demonstrated by the seven "C's," similar to or different from the goals of American schools?

6. Would this be a school you would want to attend? Why or why not?

6

Pastors Michael and Susan Thomas

Pastors Michael and Susan Thomas served the English-language congregation at Lutheran Church of the Redeemer in Jerusalem.

— This Time of Crisis Calls Out to God —

In October 2000, on the Feast Day of St. Francis of Assisi, Pastors Michael and Susan Thomas of the Evangelical Lutheran Church in America wrote this report about the violence that was happening at the outset of what would become the Second Intifada.

The past six days have witnessed terrible events in Palestine and Israel. This has meant great suffering and many deaths, almost entirely among the Palestinians. In the large things of life and in the mundane, nothing has been spared. Yet in the surreal world of the Holy Land, tour buses still disgorge their passengers in Bethlehem's Manger Square and our PTA meetings still occur.

But we are all touched. A teenage neighbor boy from Ireland told us this evening, "At first I didn't believe my Palestinian friend, that a 12-year-old boy had been shot and killed and his father shot as he tried to shield his son. I thought he was just trying to make me more sympathetic to the Palestinians. But then my mother brought home the pictures and I believed him. Who would ever do something like that? When I look at the pictures I get teary, so I don't like to look at them too much."

We are living in an abnormal situation. Jerusalem is, in essence, not a "normal" place, but it is more abnormal than usual to buy groceries and a newspaper and find yourself sobbing in the parking lot. This time of crisis calls out to God.

ELCA Presiding Bishop George Anderson and General Secretary Ishmael Noko of the Lutheran World Federation (LWF) spoke clearly to the events of the last six days. They were stunned by the Israeli army shooting stone-throwing youths on the grounds of Augusta Victoria, the LWF hospital on the Mount of Olives, only a couple of hundred yards from our house.

Bishop Munib Younan of the Evangelical Lutheran Church of Jerusalem and hospital director Craig Kippels protested to the soldiers who entered the grounds—"This should not be!" Indeed, it should not be—that a humanitarian sanctuary becomes a battleground.

Friday afternoon, September 29, at our home on the Mount of Olives overlooking the Dome of the Rock and Al-Aqsah Mosque, we first heard shouts, then shots break out, seemingly hundreds of them for many minutes just as Friday prayers were ending. Some Palestinians were killed and many were wounded. As we stood with our neighbors outside, watching the unfolding scene, we knew that something truly terrible had occurred.

Within moments, ambulances were coming and going from the Old City, carrying people to the two hospitals on the Mount of Olives, one of which was Augusta Victoria. Across the way, several cars were set on fire by angry Palestinians.

While all this was happening, our family was packing for a congregational weekend retreat on the transformative power of prayer. Torn about what to do, we decided to proceed to meet those who were driving to the retreat. Driving up the Mount of Olives, through a crowd of angry, distraught people, we knew it was serious. We passed Augusta Victoria just as the soldiers were arriving.

It seemed that a weekend of prayer made little sense, and yet, perhaps it made the best possible sense. With heavy hearts we proceeded to Tiberias with adults, students, and children. Over the next two days we came together often in prayer. We prayed fervently for those being tested, being killed. We prayed for the world, for ourselves, for our families, and especially for the Palestinian people who were suffering once again. In short, we prayed for transformation.

The trip home on Sunday from Tiberias on the shores of the Sea of Galilee, normally just a couple of hours, became an eight-hour journey. We saw for ourselves the disturbances occurring in the Israeli Arab villages along the way and were routed around them. We were delayed further by an incident at the Israeli roadblock on the perimeter of Augusta Victoria, close to our home. Tonight the violence in Gaza and elsewhere continues, and talks in Paris between Madeline Albright, Yasser Arafat, and Ehud Barak proceed. While experts may offer trenchant analyses, the truth is that no one knows what the coming days and weeks will bring. And it is not even clear what we should be praying for.

One of our members commented, "I know in the long run this evil will not prevail. I can't really pray for an end to the violence, because I know the energy for justice in this land lies underneath it. But I can pray for that energy to be channeled into strength and courage for change that is lasting and nonviolent." To affirm that such evil will not finally prevail is a statement of faith that we are more accustomed to hear in other words—such as, "I know that my Redeemer lives!" and "Who can separate us from the love of God?"

Last weekend we were very blessed by having the Christian Peacemaker Team with us. Tonight they cannot leave the small Hebron apartment where they live because of the violence. Members of our congregation living in Bethlehem feel trapped by fear of the violence. In Beit Sahour, where the shepherds heard the first news of peace to those of good will from the angels at Christ's birth, our fellow Lutherans find Israeli jeeps full of soldiers at their doors. They hear shots throughout the night in an area that is supposed to be autonomous Palestinian territory. Beit Sahour and Bethlehem have seen much bloodshed these last days. George Awad, secretary for the Evangelical Lutheran Church in Jerusalem, closes his shutters at six and tells his children, "Tonight you stay in!"

Jerusalem is quiet now—eerily so. The normally crowded streets of the Old City seem unnaturally wide as the shops are closed due to a general strike called by the Palestinians. East Jerusalem is similarly closed down. Again, it is surreal to pick up our children from the Anglican International School in West Jerusalem and see life continuing there essentially as usual. How do you live normally in an abnormal situation?

A week and a half ago Yehuda Amichai, the beloved Israeli poet, died. His poem, "I, May I Rest In Peace," ends this way:

I don't want to fulfill my parents' prophecy that life is war.
I want peace with all my body and all my soul.
Rest me in peace.

Remember the plight of the Palestinians in your prayers and the small but living Christian community in the Holy Land, especially the Evangelical Lutheran Church of Jerusalem. Pray also for strength and courage for the Israeli human rights and peace organizations. Pray for the Christian Peacemakers Team in Hebron. Indeed, pray for all the people of the Holy Land. Pray that hearts might be converted, justice done, peace made, and repentance shown. Pray individually and pray together in your congregations. Contact Churches for Middle East Peace for ways to be effective advocates for a just peace.

If you write to the Prime Minister of Israel, implore him to call back the heavy offensive weaponry, such as helicopter gunships, used these past few days, from the especially tense sites in the West Bank. Urge him to seek security in justice rather than in overpowering military force, so that both Israelis and Palestinians can live in peace and reject our "parents' prophecy that life is war." And urge Chairman Arafat to seek all available avenues for a just peace, to quell incendiary language among would-be leaders, to be dedicated to the good and welfare of all Palestinians.

Today is the day of St. Francis, famous for his prayer for peace. Monday was the anniversary of the birth of Mahatma Ghandi, the Indian leader who taught the world nonviolence. Dietrich Bonhoeffer, German Lutheran pastor and resister of the Nazi regime, wrote:

> If we are to learn what God promises . . . we must persevere in quiet meditation on the life, sayings, deeds, sufferings, and death of Jesus. It is certain that we may always live close to God and in the light of [God's] presence, and that such living is entirely new life for us . . . . It is certain that our joy is hidden in suffering, and our life in death; it is certain that in all this we are in a [community] that sustains us. (*Letters and Papers from Prison*, New York: The Macmillan Company, 1967, pp. 213-214.)

You are part of the community in which we stand. Your prayers bear up the people of this land. Do not grow weary in your prayers and witness for peace and justice for all of God's children.

❧ Encounter at Beit Jala ❧

On August 29, 2001, the Israeli Army made an incursion into the city of Beit Jala, taking up positions on the roof of the Lutheran church building, endangering the lives of the 50 children and youth who lived in the orphanage on the premises. With a full curfew imposed on the town the children were isolated there with some educators who also lived on the premises.

The closure necessitated hours of negotiations with Israeli authorities. Eventually Bishop Munib Younan, the Lutheran bishop in Jerusalem, managed to get clearance for a delegation from the church office, consisting of Lutheran clergy and international coworkers, to visit the church and bring food and other necessities to the children.

Pastors Michael and Susan Thomas sent this message to prayer supporters worldwide.

The sign by the gate of the Lutheran Church of the Reformation in Beit Jala, West Bank, yesterday afternoon, August 28, was badly damaged. "Abraham's House," it said—the sign pointed the way to an unfinished guest house begun two years ago by this Palestinian Lutheran congregation. It was to be a site for encounter among "the children of Abraham"—Jewish, Christian, and Muslim—from this land and abroad.

The long nose of the Israeli tank parked at the entrance to the church had no doubt shattered the sign, as it had helped to shatter the dream.

After hours of effort for our church delegation to be allowed into this closed, curfewed portion of Beit Jala, we stood together in the courtyard of the church premises. We were Jews, Christians, and Muslims who were indeed "having an encounter." But the Jews standing with us were Israeli peace activists. The Muslims were local press and children from the congregation's orphanage. The Christians were the rest of the boys and the staff of the boarding home, along with the Lutheran Bishop Munib Younan; the pastor of

Reformation church, Jadallah Shehada; and an array of international clergy and other representatives.

The encounter we were having was with Israeli Jewish soldiers who had entered the church compound in the early hours of the morning as part of the action of the Israeli military occupation of Palestinian-controlled Beit Jala. They had taken position in "Abraham's House" and were using it as a site for their sharpshooters, since it overlooks the village center. It may have been this very building, the one Pastor Shehada planned to use for increasing interfaith understanding in this land, that Israeli sharpshooters fired from earlier that morning when the pastor tried to come near the church.

We peered through the decorative openings in the locked metal doors and, in the dark unfinished interior, could occasionally see soldiers ascending and descending the stairs.

"What are you doing in there? You should not be here! This is a church! Come out! Go home!" several of us called to them. Unlike other occasions, when we have indeed been able to engage soldiers in conversation, these were not talking.

The reason they were not talking was that they weren't there. We knew they weren't there because we'd been told they weren't there. Bishop Munib Younan, who had been involved since the early morning in conversations with church staff trapped inside, had been assured by Israel's military commander for the Bethlehem District that there were no soldiers on the church premises.

"If you see soldiers there," the Israeli commander had offered helpfully, "please let us know."

Bishop Younan let him know. He also suggested that if the commander really didn't know his soldiers were there, then it would be wise to keep better tabs on them. And he insisted that the soldiers must leave the church premises immediately. Then the bishop gathered us to sing a hymn, "How Great Thou Art," in Arabic and in English, to pray, and to receive a blessing.

Sometimes the symbolic irony in this land and this situation is not the least bit subtle. It can turn us into cynics or humorists of the absurd, at least on the days it doesn't break our hearts. But yesterday—despite the irony and fear contained in it—was a day of inspiration and hope. The Lutheran church worldwide brought pressure on Israel via diplomatic channels; the diplomatic corps here and abroad who were told of the takeover of a church moved into action; and the U.S. State Department officially called for Israel to pull its occupying troops out of Beit Jala, mentioning that it was particularly concerned about the Lutheran orphanage there. By 8:30 P.M. yesterday the soldiers had left the church premises. It was a small victory in a larger arena of defeats.

Churches have historically served as sanctuaries. The 50 boys who have come to the boarding section of the Lutheran Church of the Reformation in Beit Jala are orphans or from broken homes. They have already sought sanctuary from their difficult lives. Now they found that sanctuary invaded. We took two of them, who had some family in Jerusalem, back to the city with us, but the rest remained behind with the orphanage staff. The question was understandably raised, "Why don't you get the boys out of there? Why don't the children leave?"

The answer is simple but it may not be so easy to understand. It is not the children who must leave. This is their home, the only real home they have. They have every right to stay. Rather, it is the occupying force that must leave. This was the principle that was so important to uphold yesterday. The children should stay. The soldiers must leave.

It is the same important principle to uphold regarding the town of Beit Jala itself, which is now under Israeli military occupation and, for that matter, regarding all of the Occupied Territories of the West Bank and Gaza.

The longer we are here and the more we observe, the more convinced we become that only when the illegal Israeli occupation ends will there be hope for safe and secure places for all. Only then can respected sanctuaries for children and adults alike be maintained on both sides.

Until then, the sanctuaries in this land are like moments in time. Even seemingly safe places, such as Reformation Lutheran Church, can be invaded and transformed into battlegrounds. Yesterday we were privileged, in the company of Bishop Younan and some of Abraham's children, to enter one of those sanctuary moments and find a blessing.

⸺ Of Caves and Graves and Job's Cactus ⸺

In November 2001, as the congregations and communities of the West Bank experienced repeated closures, the people under virtual house arrest, Pastor Susan Thomas preached this sermon.

One Friday afternoon, I drove from Jerusalem to Bethlehem for the biweekly English-language worship at Christmas Lutheran Church. On the drive, we passed a burned-out building. "What happened to it?" our 16-year-old son asked with some alarm. "How did it burn?"

Although he is very aware of the conflict in this land, my son had not been to Bethlehem for many months. We stopped to gaze at the damage for a few minutes and he noted with irony the name still visible on a sign: "Paradise Hotel."

Two weeks ago Pastor Sandra Olewine, who lives in Bethlehem and serves as pastoral associate at Christmas Lutheran and as the United Methodist liaison to Jerusalem, called to tell us not to come for the scheduled worship. It was too dangerous, she said, because we would have to come directly through the line of fire to get to Christmas Church.

And no one was venturing out anyway during the Israeli military incursion. A small community of four was living at the church. One has an apartment there and others, including Sandra, had taken shelter in the church compound. So they would pray on their own, knowing that we were praying with them here in Jerusalem.

When we began these regular prayers in Bethlehem at the beginning of September, we prepared for this eventuality. The normal practice would be for the pastors and some people from Redeemer Lutheran in Jerusalem to visit, but when it was difficult or unwise to try to get across the checkpoint into Bethlehem, Pastor Sandra would already be there to lead.

Last Friday I had planned to depart from our usual format of reading one of the assigned texts for the coming Sunday as the focus for our reflection. Instead, I had chosen a text from the previous Sunday's All Saints service. It was Hebrews 11:32—12:2, the text referring to the suffering of the saints, part of the great cloud of witnesses, who:

> through faith . . . administered justice, obtained promises, . . . quenched raging fire, escaped the edge of the sword, won strength out of weakness, . . . put foreign armies to flight . . . suffered . . . chains and imprisonment. They were stoned to death, . . . killed by the sword; . . . destitute . . . They wandered in deserts and mountain, and in caves and holes in the ground.

At the All Saints service, these words about the saints living in caves and holes in the ground had jumped out at me. I knew that those with whom we would be worshiping in Bethlehem had spent a goodly part of the recent Israeli invasion in caves and holes in the ground, including Sandra at Christmas Church. And the entire Zoughbi family, with their four young children and assorted others, who had retreated to the cave under their home, where Mr. Zoughbi, in fact, was born.

So Hebrews text was very appropriate, especially as our regular site for worship is a Bethlehem cave, one of the caves beneath Christmas Lutheran Church.

But perhaps when undergoing hardship, Scripture speaks with renewed relevance. For the upcoming text from Job would not be denied its place among Christians gathered in that Bethlehem cave. It was this text that finally spoke most urgently to our life together in this land:

> O that my words were written down! O that they were inscribed in a book! O that with an iron pen and with lead they were engraved on a rock forever! For I know that my Redeemer lives, and that at the last he will stand upon the earth; and after my skin has been thus destroyed, then in my flesh I shall see God, whom I shall see on my side, and my eyes shall behold, and not another. Job 19:23-27a

Many of us here can identify with Job's cry, "O that my words were written down!" Living in this situation, there is an intense and urgent need to speak. Some of us do that regularly, writing as part of our work or out of the conviction that others need to understand and take seriously what is happening here. Certainly the people living and working in Bethlehem have been doing this. Members of the staff of the International Center of Bethlehem have posted personal stories about life during the incursion on the center's Web site.

Most of us write in ephemeral media, including the journalists. Radio and newspaper reports are, of course, seldom retained, although effective in the moment. E-mail messages or Internet reports, which most of us use, have a similar fleeting lifespan, although we pray they are read and digested.

So Job's plea for permanence for his words is well understood among us. Job wants his words inscribed in a book, or, better yet, written with lead poured into incised letters on a rock, which would last forever. Clearly, he thinks what he has to say is important.

These words come when Job had suffering behind him and suffering yet ahead of him. He already had lost his wealth, his children, and his health; he has had to endure the ineffective and even blasphemous consolations of his friends. And there is no relief in sight. The aftermath of what has happened to him just keeps on unfolding. He's in the middle of it. Behind and ahead of him is suffering. The end of it is not near.

In that Bethlehem cave, heads nodded in recognition. Like Job, we and the people of this land are not at the beginning nor at the end of the suffering. We are in the middle of it. And what can we say in the middle of it? What words would we want inscribed now in permanent ink or with metal in rock?

These were Job's words: "I know that my Redeemer lives, and that at the last he will stand upon the earth." Though my very skin be destroyed, Job went on to say, I know that I will see my Redeemer standing next to me. This one—and no other. It will be a day of vindication, a day full of grace.

Oddly enough, it is the ephemeral medium of music composed more than a millennium after Job's words were written that has assisted in making these words last. One of the most beautiful and hope-filled arias of Handel's *Messiah* is "I know that my Redeemer liveth . . . " and it uses these words spoken from the middle of Job's suffering.

Job's words have been inscribed in the hearts and memories of millions of people through this music. Not grasped and held, but felt. The faith they proclaim has been understood at a level deeper than the few millimeters of depth that might be incised on a rock.

What these words say to us now is this: It is in the very middle of suffering that the Christian community must most faithfully proclaim the resurrection of Christ. I say this knowing that the book of Job was written long before Jesus lived; I say it knowing that this particular scriptural text is very corrupt; that is, it is full of ambiguity of meaning. And that the book of Job itself is a literary narrative, albeit a narrative of faith.

Nonetheless, the experience holds. Coming into the center of suffering, speaking out of cave or hole in the ground, a hole that is too reminiscent of a grave, there is nothing more important to say than "I know that my Redeemer live—this one, and no other."

Zoughbi Zoughbi, born in the cave where his family recently took shelter, spoke about this text on Friday. He said that in Arabic, as in English, there is a common phrase: "the patience of Job." The word *patience* in Arabic is the same as the word for cactus.

He described the tough and thorny outer skin of the cactus, which protects the sweet nourishing flesh inside. The cactus is patient, waiting and storing the water it needs to remain soft in its heart. Now it is the hearts of the people that Zoughbi worries about, that they might remain soft hearts of flesh, not tough and thorny.

Inside the tough protection of those cave walls on Friday, I pray that ours were hearts of flesh, soft and nourishing, filled with the moisture of God's tears and God's love falling over this tough, dry land.

The patience of Job, the soft heart of the cactus, and the proclamation of the living Redeemer—these were our lessons from Christians gathered in a Bethlehem cave, listening for the word of God.

From that tomb-like place came Alleluias, came the assurance that Christ is risen, came a day full of grace.

Questions for reflection and discussion

1. Once started, violence almost always escalates—it rarely dissipates on its own. Someone has to make a move to change its course. How can that happen? What could a Christian do to stop violence?

2. Do you know violence when you see it? What are the different types of violence you have read about in these essays?

3. Francis of Assisi prayed this way, "Lord, make me an instrument of your peace." The term "instrument" suggests more than just agreement or being okay with peace. Make a list of the qualities of someone who is an "instrument" of peace.

4. What is a sanctuary? Describe what it means for a place to be safe.

5. Tell about a safe place you have known.

6. No one should have to hide or fear in their home—or their home country. Do you have a right to be free of fear in your home? Does everyone have that right? How could you take steps to ensure that right for yourself and others?

7. What would a "sanctuary moment" be like?

8. *Curfew* and *Closure*—these words appear in the news all the time, but do you know what they mean? *Closure* means no one can move in or out of your town or your neighborhood. *Curfew* means "house arrest" for everyone and it lasts for days and days. No one can leave their house, for any reason, at risk of being shot. What do you think about this?

9. Until peace comes, our hope must be in the promises of Jesus. In experiences of suffering, what are the ways we can most faithfully proclaim the resurrection of Jesus Christ?

Resources

Books

Armstrong, Karen. 1996. *Jerusalem: One City, Three Faiths.* New York: Balantine Books. A British religious scholar provides an account of Jerusalem's 5,000-year history.

Ashrawi, Hanan. 1995. *This Side of Peace: A Personal Account.* New York: Simon and Schuster. An insider's view of Middle East diplomacy.

Ateek, Naim Stifan. 1989. *Justice and Only Justice: A Palestinian Theology of Liberation.* Maryknoll, NY: Orbis Books. A Jerusalem pastor presents a theology for Palestinian Christians.

Bennis, Phyllis. 2002. *Understanding the Palestinian-Israeli Conflict: A Primer.* Orlando, FL: TARI (Trans-Arab Research Institute, Inc., PO Box 691944, Orlando, FL 32869-1944). This resource, which includes maps, answers the most common questions regarding the complex conflict between Palestine and Israel.

Burge, Gary M. 2003. *Whose Land? Whose Promise? What Christians Are Not Being Told About Israel.* Pilgrim Press.

Chacour, Elias. 1984. *Blood Brothers.* Grand Rapids, MI: Chosen Books. This is a memoir of childhood expulsion from Galilee in 1947.

Chacour, Elias and Mary E. Jensen. 2000. *We Belong to the Land.* Univerity of Notre Dame Press. The authors explore what Palestine means to its Christian poplulation.

Chapman, Colin Gilbert. 2002. *Whose Promised Land? The Continuing Crisis over Israel and Palestine.* Grand Rapids, Mich.: Baker Books. Chapman explores the complex issues surrounding the promised land.

Cragg, Kenneth. 1991. *Arab Christian: A History in the Middle East.* Louisville, KY: Westminster Press. Cragg discusses Christianity in the Middle East and its relationship to Islam.

Hass, Amira. (Elana Wesley and Maxine Kaufman-Lacusta, translators). 1996. *Drinking the Sea at Gaza: Days and Nights in a Land Under Siege.* New York: Henry Holt and Company. An Israeli journalist living under siege tells the story of the Palestinian people.

Kaltner, John. 2003. *Islam: What Non-Muslims Should Know.* Minneapolis: Fortress Press, 2003. Kaltner clarifies Islamic beliefs and practices.

McGowan, Daniel A. and Marc H. Ellis (editors). 1998. *Remembering Deir Yassin: The Future of Israel and Palestine.* Northampton, MA: Olive Branch Press. Recollections of the 1948 massacre of Palestinians.

Neff, Donald. 1998. *Fifty Years of Israel.* Washington: American Educational Trust. A compilation of the author's "Middle East History" columns.

Raheb, Mitri. 1995. *I Am a Palestinian Christian.* Minneapolis: Fortress Press. The continuing plight of Palestinian Christians told by a Lutheran pastor in Bethlehem.

Said, Edward W. 1997. *Covering Islam: How the Media and the Experts Determine How We See the Rest of the World* (revised edition). New York: Random House. A critical look at how American media sources prejudice Americans against Islamic people.

Shabbas, Audrey (editor). 1998. *The Arab World Studies Notebook.* Berkeley, CA: AWAIR. (Email to order: awair@igc.apc.org) This is a basic resource for teaching about the Arab world for all ages.

Wagner, Donald E. 1995. *Anxious for Armageddon: A Call to Partnership for Middle Eastern and Western Christians.* Scottsdale, PA: Herald Press. An Evangelical Christian shares his involvement in the Palestinian-Israeli conflict.

Wagner, Donald E. 2001. *Dying in the Land of Promise: Palestine and Palestinian Christianity from Pentecost to 2000.* London: Melisende. The history of and the unique roles for Palestinian Christians today.

Web sites

www.elca.org/middleeast "Middle East Connections" is from the Evangelical Lutheran Church in America.

www.cmep.org Churches for Middle East Peace.

www.pepm.org Peaceful Ends through Peaceful Means

www.holyland-lutherans.org The Evangelical Lutheran Church in Jerusalem.

www.annadwa.org International Center of Bethlehem (Lutheran).

www.rapprochement.org Peace center in Beit Sahour, West Bank.

www.btselem.org Israeli human rights organization.

www.sabeel.org Sabeel, the Ecumenical Liberation Theology Center in Jerusalem.

OTHER LUTHERAN VOICES TITLES

Large-quantity purchases or custom editions of these books are available at a discount from the publisher. For more information, contact the sales department at Augsburg Fortress, Publishers, 1-800-328-4648, or write to: Sales Director, Augsburg Fortress, Publishers, P.O. Box 1209, Minneapolis, MN 55440-1209.

See www.lutheranvoices.com

DATE

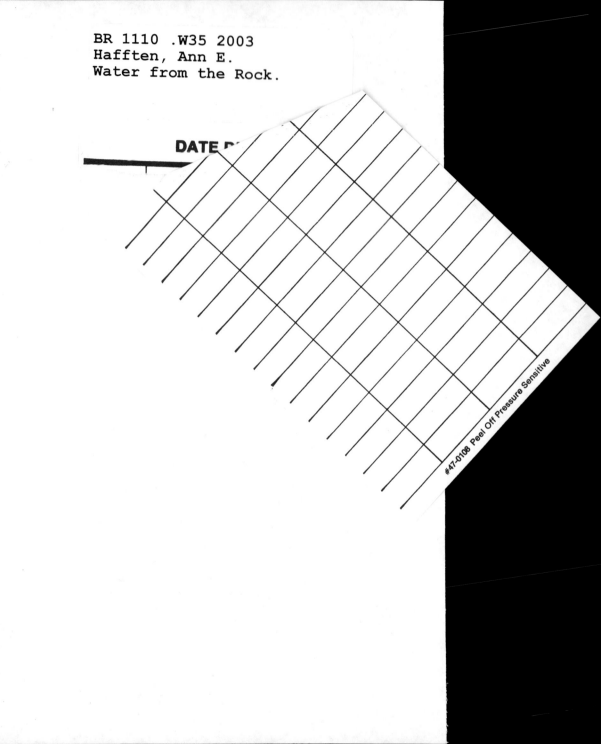

#47-0108 Peel Off Pressure Sensitive